FROM "WHO AM I?"
TO
"HOW WILL I KNOW WHEN TO GIVE TO OTHERS
AND WHEN TO SAY 'NO'?"

THE PORTABLE THERAPIST ENCOURAGES YOU
TO DISCOVER . . .

- Why western culture's "Doing" Model has given you "crazy" training . . . and how to find an alternative

- What will help you eliminate the unnecessary pain of the "trauma drama" of everyday life

- Why having illusions, expectations, dreams, and wishes is dangerous . . . and how they waste your time

- What is the secret of your inner child

- What two prevalent and destructive illusions are usually held when you enter a relationship

- What are the only two things in the entire world within your control

- How you can fall out of love when a relationship ends

- The three answers to the question "If I change, will my partner?"

- How to be a hero

CARING ANSWERS TO ESSENTIAL QUESTIONS . . .
A THERAPEUTIC APPROACH TO DEEPENING AWARENESS
AND LIVING FULLY NOW

By Susanna McMahon

The Portable Problem Solver:
Having Healthy Relationships

The Portable Problem Solver:
Coping with Life's Stressors

the
Portable
Therapist

Susanna McMahon, Ph.D.

A Dell Trade Paperback

A DELL TRADE PAPERBACK

Published by
Dell Publishing
a division of
Bantam Doubleday Dell Publishing Group, Inc.
1540 Broadway
New York, New York 10036

Library of Congress Cataloging in Publication Data

McMahon, Susanna.
   The portable therapist / Susanna McMahon.
      p.   cm.
   Originally published: Houston, Tex. : Jencat Publications, 1992.
   Includes bibliographical references.
   ISBN 0-440-50603-4
   1. Self-esteem. 2. Psychotherapy—Popular works.
3. Interpersonal relations. 4. Conduct of life. I. Title.
RC489.S43M36 1994
158'.1—dc20   93-30957/CIP

Printed in the United States of America
Published simultaneously in Canada
August 1994
20 19 18 17 16 15 14 13 12
BVG

PENN BOOKS
1 PENN PLAZA
NEW YORK NY 10119
(212) 239-0311

SALES RECEIPT

2/19/01 4:07:56 PM Reg :1 TX1D: 93200

Misc. Item Taxable Item	
QTY: 1 @ $10.95	$10.95
SubTotal:	$10.95
Sales Tax 8.25%:	$0.90
Amount Due:	$11.85
Cash Sale:	$11.85
Change Due:	$0.00

For Buzz

Acknowledgments

This book is based on a life's accumulation of data, and therefore it is very difficult to thank everyone who contributed to it. There are very few references to others, not because they do not exist, but because I cannot be precise in crediting each idea or concept to the first person who thought of it. Because there are so many people to thank for what I have learned from them, I hope it suffices to thank everyone that I know.

I especially must give thanks to my clients. Each client that I have had has taught me so much. Thank you most of all for your trust as we stumbled along together toward the answers. Thank you for forgiving the mistakes that I made and for sticking with the business of getting healthy. Particularly I want to thank those of you who did get healthy for confirming that it is possible. You gave me the confidence to write this book. You practiced what I preached and you showed me that the ideas presented here do work. You fired me and became your own therapists. You taught me that therapy can be brief and effective.

I also want to thank Timothy for his loving support; he lives Social Interest naturally. Elizabeth Haas and Marcia Grant were my first readers in Madrid, and their reinforcement and help were invaluable and much appreciated. In Houston, Art and Janet Jago were equally supportive and helpful and equally appreciated. Tom O'Daniel, Art Francia, and David Dean helped me with the format and technical issues of getting this book off the computer screen and onto the written page and I thank them for saving me hours of work. I thank my mother for beginning it all and my daughters, Jennifer, Kelly, and Catherine, for believing in me and loving the book. Finally, I wish to thank my agent, Margret McBride, and my editor, Trish Todd at Dell, for being so enthusiastic and for their efforts in getting *The Portable Therapist* to publication.

 **Contents**

II. Conceptual Issues

III. Individual Issues

IV. Relationship Issues

V. The End

Introduction

I wrote this book for you, the person who knows that there are answers out there but frequently seems overwhelmed by the questions. I wrote this book for those of you who are functioning, who are doing what you think you are supposed to be doing but are somehow missing out on something. You get up every morning, do your work, attend to hundreds of small details, drop into bed exhausted each night, and when you do have a few minutes, you find yourself contemplating what life is about. This book is for those of you who are expert "doers" but have somehow lost the art of being. This book is also for those of you who know something about being but need some help and encouragement toward life enhancement.

I wrote this book for those of you who have never read a self-help book before because you do not believe that the answers to your life problems can be found by reading a book. I agree with you; solutions do not follow from merely reading a book. The answer to the question "Why don't the self-help books work for me?" on page 59 explains why reading any book is not enough. Some of you may never have read a self-help book because you feel that no one else could understand your problems as no one else is you, living your life and feeling your feelings. This is true, but while we do not share specific circumstances and traumatic details, we do share our feelings about what bothers us. As humans, we can all relate to sadness and loss, anger and frustration, feelings of worthlessness and discouragement. This relating can be shared and this process of sharing teaches us that we are not alone and that we can belong. If this is your first self-help book, I hope that you will find that it does pertain to you and that you can use the answers in this book to find your own answers, to encourage you in your search for your worth and your esteem and to increase your personal sense of belongingness.

I also wrote this book for those of you who read every self-help book that comes on the market because you believe that there is a secret out there to living your life, and if you can only find the right book you will find your personal secret. I will not presume that this is the right book with your secret. I will, however, direct you to the section dealing with the concept of paradox. The paradox of finding the secret that unlocks the meaning of life is that there is no secret. The information is out there, it has been out there for as long as we have recorded history and it is accessible through many channels. At the heart of all religions, all philosophies, all doctrines concerned with the meaning of life and all psychology lies the meaning of existence: Be true to yourself. Love yourself. Recognize your own worth and goodness. These are simple concepts but they are not easy to implement. The proliferation of self-help books attests to the fact that being oneself is not something that naturally occurs in our culture. Unfortunately, Self-Esteem cannot be given you by someone else. The philosophy of self-love may sound simple but the process of acquiring self-worth is not an easy one. This book recognizes your search, your quest for the meaning of your life, and, hopefully, will function as an encouragement in your journey. We may read the right answer one hundred times before we "get it" but the only answer that is relevant is that last one that we finally understand. Keep reading, keep working, keep trying. I sincerely hope that this book helps you in your search and your discovery of your personal worth.

I wrote this book for the person who is balanced, emotionally healthy, and loaded with Self-Esteem. We can never have enough encouragement in this crazy, discouraging world. We need all the reinforcement that we can get. Because Self-Esteem is a process and not a fixed goal, every day brings new challenges, difficult confrontations, and pain and loss which deplete our feelings of worth and self-love. How easy it is to forget all the problems that we have already solved when confronted with a new one. How easy it becomes to lose faith and hope in ourselves when our external world seems to be falling apart. How very difficult it is to love yourself when no one around seems to love you. How natural it feels to berate yourself when you make a mistake. This book is about learning to encourage yourself and to be kind to yourself when your world is in chaos. Recognizing that Self-Esteem is process and not commodity is a critical component of this book. Because it is process, we can never have enough. We will always need encouraging reminders, support, and positive reinforcements. I hope this book will function as a reminder for those of you who have already discovered your own self-worth.

I also wrote this book for those of you who have never understood the concept of Self-Esteem and the value of loving yourself. You may have heard the words before but you never personally grasped the concept. Maybe you were too busy or too involved with playing at life, but somehow you missed it. Maybe you thought the idea of loving yourself was too simple or too esoteric; maybe you felt that taking care of your own needs, belonging, and feeling good were selfish and part of the *me* generation. You were trained to play it by the straight and narrow and you wanted to be a good student and follow the rules of society. These rules dictate that if you do what most of those around you tell you to do, which is to try for perfection, be altruistic, work hard, and do the right thing, then you will be okay. So you have followed their guidelines but somehow, some way, you are not okay. Something is wrong, something is missing, and perhaps you are even afraid to admit this. You do not even know where to begin to fix your life. It is difficult to acknowledge that your life does not work for you. But when you are alone and the facade is down, you are confused and vulnerable. Read this book. You are not alone and you are not in such a bad place. Confusion and uncertainty are excellent beginning points for discovery, growth, and change. I hope this book will convince you that finding your own meaning, your own self-worth, your own goodness is a worthwhile endeavor for you to try. It is your life and you are the only one who can live it meaningfully.

Above all, I wrote this book because I had to. I wrote this book as a reminder to myself to practice what I teach. I chose a question-and-answer format because it most closely resembles the therapeutic process that occurs with clients. There are no case studies mentioned in *The Portable Therapist,* not because they do not exist—every question in this book brings to mind many clients who have asked it—but because I wanted the reader to have a more personal involvement with the answers. When you are interested in a specific question, you will fill in your own details and apply the answer to your own situation. Each of you has your own reasons for asking the question, each of you has your own story to tell and each of you will decide what to do, if anything, with the information given in the answers. I hope that this book works for you. I hope that the questions are relevant questions for you personally and that the answers lead you toward self-insight and awareness of your tremendous worth and goodness.

There is an underlying philosophy in *The Portable Therapist.* It is not an original philosophy; it is not a complex or even a difficult philosophy. This philosophy is simply that *you are good* and your goodness is within you always. You do not have to *do* anything to be good, you cannot work toward being good and you cannot earn this goodness. It is already there. The work that is involved is to acknowledge your goodness, believe in yourself, and trust that the best that you can be is centered by your own goodness. In other words, being good is given; living goodness is the difficult task. Paradoxically, it takes even more hard work and effort to negate this goodness, to become truly evil. We have not been trained to acknowledge ourselves as good. We have been trained to criticize, judge, and denigrate ourselves as if we are not good. Because our training has been so pervasive and comprehensive, it can be frightening to recognize this goodness within. It can feel strange and uncomfortable. But it also feels liberating and very powerful. If you are in doubt, try this little experiment. Close your eyes and say to yourself: "I am good. I am good. I am good." Keep saying this until you begin to feel something. You may feel like crying, you may feel somewhat afraid, you may find this difficult to say and believe. The better your training, the more difficult the exercise. Stay with it until you feel something. Acknowledging your own goodness will feel right. It will feel powerful and it will affect you. Recognizing your inner goodness is the first step toward Self-Esteem.

The Portable Therapist also has an underlying psychological theory. Again, this theory is not original. It is called *Natural High* and was developed by Walter "Buzz" O'Connell. Dr. O'Connell, influenced by the works of Alfred Adler, believes that Natural High occurs when one has both *Self-Esteem* and *Social Interest*. All of these terms are explained fully within this book. In brief, however, this theory means that by having self-love and loving relationships with others, we will feel universal belongingness. We will have found meaning, worth, and value, and we will feel joy at being alive. Isn't that what we all really want and strive toward?

This book grew out of ten years of doing therapy. I began my clinical practice at the Veterans Administration (VA) Hospital in

Houston, Texas. I was fortunate to work for several years with Vietnam veterans suffering from Post Traumatic Stress Disorder. From them I learned so much, but the most important concept they taught me is that life is not fair. It just isn't. They also showed me that doing what you have to do to survive can result in devastation to one's self-concept unless you can learn to forgive. Because life is not fair, the concept of perfect does not work. We can never be perfect and therefore it is critical that we can forgive—ourselves first and then others. Fortunately, we can learn forgiveness and we can get on with our lives no matter what has happened to us. My work with drug addicts, alcoholics, and severely disturbed patients also confirmed the need for forgiveness and the trainability of this concept.

From the VA, I moved to Germany and worked as a child psychologist for the U.S. Army. My young clients, particularly the sexually abused ones, taught me that bad things do happen to good people and that, in some way, we are all victims. Even more importantly, I learned that we are all survivors and we need to acknowledge and reward ourselves for surviving. These children, and their families, showed me that goodness and self-love are internal attributes and not removed by external traumas. They also taught me that character grows out of pain and loss.

The idea for *The Portable Therapist* occurred while I was working as the director of the Community Mental Health Program in Madrid, Spain. Many of my clients in Madrid were successful, high-functioning, and intelligent expatriates. From these clients I learned that success cannot be externally defined. Doing and having do not result in a joyous, balanced, and complete life. These clients taught me the need for a redefinition of success and the even greater need for self-encouragement and the provision of meaningful internal rewards. My belief in short-term therapy was confirmed by the successes of these clients in Madrid.

This book is not designed to be a substitute for therapy. There are times in all our lives when we need outside support, guidance, and an objective perspective. The questions listed are serious questions. All of them have been asked and dealt with by clients in great pain and confusion. The answers given to the questions are brief. They may sound simple but they are not meant to diminish the intensity or severity of the problem or issue being confronted. They were designed to be indicators toward finding solutions for the problems or, when no solutions exist, helping to learn how to cope with the problem. If these answers are enough to encourage, redirect, and help the reader problem-solve, wonderful. I would hope that readers who need more help with their problems will find in the answer the encouragement to seek out that help. This book was written for functioning adults. It will not be enough for severely disturbed people or those with serious traumas or personality disorders. It will not function as a "quick fix" as I do not believe there is such a thing.

The Portable Therapist was not designed to be read through quickly and then put on the shelf. Rather, it was written so that each question can be read as needed. This book contains eighty-three questions and answers which have been arranged into four main sections. The underlying theory and all relevant terms have been explained in the first section, which I have called the philosophical section because these questions deal with the "larger" or more global issues in our lives. I would recommend reading this section first in order to understand the terms which occur throughout the book. The second section is conceptual and deals with the theory and practice of learning Self-Esteem. Personal or individual problems are covered in the third section. The fourth section, explaining Social Interest, deals with relationships and their issues. The definition of Natural High occurs in the very last question in the book. The reader may note that over three fourths of the book is devoted to learning Self-Esteem and only one fourth deals with Social Interest. Natural High is covered only by the last question.

This format is intentional because the learning of Self-Esteem is critical to the development of Social Interest, and the Natural High occurs once you have both Self-Esteem and Social Interest. The list of suggested readings at the end of this book are works that either directly contributed to concepts mentioned in *The Portable Therapist* or that will provide more information on specific topics of interest to the reader.

As mentioned, all the answers in this book are brief and basically simple. I will anticipate the criticism of being overly simplistic and superficial which is often given to brief therapies. I do not believe that a short or a simple answer is superficial *if* the client or reader internalizes the message. No therapist can give any answer, no matter what the length or difficulty level, that will produce change unless the client or reader relates with the information given and uses this new knowledge to change themselves. It has been my experience that basic, simple but relevant answers are used and internalized more frequently than complex ones. Each reader will choose what answers make sense to them personally and each will decide what information to retain and to use toward their own change and growth. This must be an individual process. Each of us discovers who we are, what is important, and how to be balanced, complete, and at peace for ourselves alone. However, this does not mean that we have to do this work by ourselves alone. We share some essential commonalities in our quest for inner peace and meaning. For example, knowing your story and what worked and did not work for you will not produce change in me but it may help me to produce my own change. Your change may give me permission, help, and encouragement to undertake my change. We learn, we grow, we change, and we share. There would be very little challenge or joy in developing Self-Esteem in a vacuum. Loving ourselves will always lead toward loving others. Loving ourselves and others will lead to joy and universal belonging, the Natural High.

The book was named *The Portable Therapist* for two reasons. The first is that a book is something portable; we can carry it with us wherever we go. The second reason is that each of us carries with us what we need wherever we go. In other words, each of us has the power to be our own therapists. We are the only ones who can take the answers that we need and make them work for us, wherever we may be, at whatever time. Each of us has the responsibility for our own lives. Each of us is ultimately our own best therapist. If we are good therapists, we will be encouraging, forgiving, supportive, sometimes nurturing and, when needed, tough toward ourselves. I hope this book will help you be a good portable therapist for yourself.

I. Philosophical Issues

❧ Who am I?

This question may be considered *the* question of our existence. It may be answered on many levels, as any answer would contain some combination of philosophical, ethical, spiritual, or behavioral perspectives. We are, in part, our training and experience, in part, our hopes and accomplishments and failures and, in part, connected to some higher power or life force. We know we have body, mind, and soul and we often ask this question in reference to one of these aspects of ourselves. We tend to define ourselves in terms of how we look, what we think and know, how we feel, and what we do. Usually, we have difficulty in combining all our parts into a cohesive whole.

When this question is asked in therapy, there is always some pain. The therapeutic answer must go beyond the externals—the roles that each of us assume, our physical appearance, our education, our status and financial worth, our ability to relate with others, and so on—to the underlying reason for asking this question. Almost always, the motivation for questioning who you are is related to the amount of insecurity that you feel. Insecurity is at the heart of all emotional dysfunctions and is highly correlated to physical ailments and spiritual anxieties. Insecurity means doubting yourself which, in turn, produces the inability to trust who and what you are which then results in not knowing yourself. If you do not know and you do not trust, how can you love? Insecurity then can be defined as low or no *Self-Esteem,* as Self-Esteem implies loving the self.

Most of us search for the answer to "who am I?" by looking for the differences between ourselves and others. We compare, we criticize, we judge, and we wonder why we feel so lost. The answers to finding ourselves, paradoxically, occur when we find the similarities we share with others. This is *Social Interest.* The more you can relate to the sameness you share with someone else, the more belongingness you can feel. The more encouragement you give and take, the more security you achieve.

Therefore, the antidotes to the reasons for asking this first question are found in the development of Self-Esteem and Social Interest. The ways and means to develop these two attributes will be found in the answers to the following questions.

What is the meaning of life?

The only way to deal with this question therapeutically rather than philosophically is to qualify the question to either "What is the meaning of my life?" or "What is the meaning of life for me?" By personalizing the question, we have changed it significantly from something abstract and out of our control to something more concrete and manageable for ourselves. Each of us now has a choice about what we consider important and how we prioritize the essentials of our own life.

The meaning of our life, because of its subjective nature, must be found within each person. The answer cannot be found in the externals. It cannot be found in another person. Unfortunately, it cannot be handed to us, either in book form or in therapy. The best that another person can do is to function as a guide, to point out new directions and perhaps provide some new materials which may lead to insight. Others may help us learn new perspectives and present choices that we may not have thought of by ourselves.

The answer to discovering the meaning of your life lies in the exploration of yourself. You give meaning to your life. The unexplored life is not a life; at best, it is only part of a life. This exploration of yourself—your life—well may be your life's work. It is difficult, painful, and requires great courage. In order to explore who you are and what your life is about, you must be willing to acquire objective "eyes" to really see yourself. This means that you must let go of the myths, illusions, and expectations that have accompanied you and helped you avoid the pain of living. You must be willing to "ride the pain" and to drop your defenses. This is hard work, and like most explorations, involves commitment, encouragement, and energy. Along the way you will learn the art of loving—first, toward yourself and, later, toward others. The result of this exploration of yourself and your life is that you will learn the art of being whole, of being balanced. All aspects of you —mental, emotional, spiritual, and interactive—are in harmony and work together. You become more at peace with yourself and with your world.

In the process of exploring your life, it helps to begin by looking for the meanings of life in the small, everyday acts of courage that are always present. Recognizing that life is lived in the moment, the here and now, and not in the past or future also helps. It takes an act of courage to stop "time jumping" from past to future and to stay focused in the present. Changing the idea that time is replaceable and money is not to the exact opposite and then living accordingly also requires courage, as you will be going against the teachings of our western world.

The meaning of life is found in the understanding of the concepts of *paradox, practice,* and *humor.* Life is paradoxical, on all levels, and this concept is explained in the next question. The best approach to understanding practice is to use the metaphor of the theater: This life is the rehearsal for what is to follow. And rehearsals are process which allows making mistakes in order to learn. If you are lucky and have good direction, you will receive encouragement while you are learning. But unlike the theater, we do not know when the final performance will occur. The rehearsing—the process—becomes our performance. Living means practicing just as life means process. The third concept, humor, provides the bridge that allows us to live with the contradictions of life and death, sanity and insanity, good and evil. By using humor, by laughing at ourselves and with others, we can learn that life is not that serious, not that important, and not unbearable.

What is the meaning of paradox?

Throughout the preceding answers, the term paradox has been frequently mentioned. The dictionary definition of *paradox* is: "A statement that seems contradictory, unbelievable or absurd but that may actually be true in fact. Something inconsistent with common experience." *(Webster's New World Dictionary)* We can also add that an occurrence opposite from one's expectations is a paradox.

Everything about living well seems to be paradoxical to what we have been trained to believe. For example, we are trained to believe that it is wrong or dangerous to love ourselves and that no one else will love us if we do love ourselves. This is paradoxical because the better we are able to love ourselves, the more love we generate for others and the more love we receive from others. Likewise, the more we take care of our own needs and wants, the more others want to be around us and offer to help us. Incidentally, the more that you caretake others to the exclusion of yourself, which is what we have been trained to do, the more resentment we foster in both ourselves and in those being caretaken. Another paradox: the more secure you feel about yourself, the more open and vulnerable you can be around others, the more power others give you. We are taught that we have to defend and protect ourselves, that we cannot appear vulnerable or others will take advantage of us. Actually, the opposite occurs.

The easiest and fastest way to understand paradox is through the use of humor. Laugh at yourself and with others. Do not take anything that seriously. It is all a game and we are all players. The best we can be occurs when we let go and have fun and play the game spontaneously. This is the paradox of life. Enjoy it.

What makes the world so crazy?

We are living in a time when the numbers of people who exhibit serious problems with life exceed the numbers who are living well. Perhaps it is time to turn from perceiving the individuals as the problem and refocus on their training. The world is crazy because we have had crazy training in how to be, how to live, and what is important. Our western culture has adopted a model which can be thought of as a *Doing* Model. It can be conceptualized as a straight line because it is clearly linear in focus. It is work-related, as it comes from the early American work ethic, and the model is oriented toward achieving goals and gaining external rewards. The beginning of the model—the straight line—is birth and then each step forward is marked by achievements. Each step forward means obtaining something new, a degree, a promotion, a marriage, a bigger house, more cars, more wealth, and on and on. Each step can be quickly compared to the one before, which is less, and to the one ahead, which is more. There is always another goal to reach until one gets to the end, which is not death but retirement. Then this model stops, as it is not interested in life without work. This model implies that life is work.

The very nature of this model, as determined from its underlying philosophy, means that this is a competitive, judgmental, achievement-oriented, and externally rewarded system for living. The problem is that this may be a model for one aspect of life, the career focus for the person, but it is a terrible model for all aspects of life. It seems that this is what has happened: we have generalized one model to cover all of life. We have become goal-oriented, competitive, judgmental, externally focused, and lost-without-work in our spiritual, emotional, interactive, and physical spheres. No wonder the world feels so crazy and we feel so lost.

What is needed is to stop blaming ourselves for inappropriate training and to begin utilizing another model for living. Far eastern philosophies and religions have developed a centuries-old model which can be conceived as a Model of *Being*. Think of this model as a circle which spirals inward without any beginning or end. There is no "better" place to be on this model. Just being on it is enough. As a matter of fact, *being* is enough. Because it is circular, this model continually recycles, meaning that you return to where you have been before, but because it spirals inward, you are never in exactly the same place as before. You are constantly changing, and everything you perceive is seen as if for the first time with your changed eyes. Because there is no known end, there can be no goal in getting to the end. Thus, the journey is the goal. It is being on the path, not the final destination, that is important. And there is no competition because where you are on the model is where you are and not comparable to where anyone else is. There is no judgment because there is no one judging. This, then, becomes the model of acceptance.

The western Model of Doing is a paradoxical model in that most people hope to achieve goals that are not obtainable with the model. The goals of peace and balance and inner power are found with the far eastern Model of Being, which is not the goal-oriented model.

The Model of Being requires some training because it is the opposite of the more familiar Doing Model. However, this far eastern model does not need to be the only model in your life. You can use the western Doing Model for some areas of your life, such as education and career advancement, and use the Being Model for the rest of your life. One warning: use of the Being Model can become addictive in a very positive manner. A certain amount of trust and a small leap of faith are required to jump off the Doing Model and experience the other. Remember, you can always jump back. You can always choose to go back to what you know. But first, please ask yourself if it worked for you. Do you know what you need to know to stop the craziness? If the answer is no, take the leap.

Why is there so much pain?

Life is full of pain. There is no place or time that has been without suffering. It is a fact of life that we are born into pain, live in pain, and die surrounded by pain. And even if we are not feeling pain ourselves we are causing pain to others. The very nature of life creates the need for pain. There can be no life without pain—not as we know life.

When this question is asked, the therapeutic answer is, however, not the philosophical one just given. What is really being asked is: "Why can't I accept the pain of living?" Or, "Why am I so afraid of the pain?"

The Doing Model, referred to in a previous question, does not teach acceptance of anything. Rather, it implies that everything can be achieved by doing more or doing better. It implies that: 1) your destiny is in your control and therefore you are responsible for what is happening to you and around you, 2) if you are in pain, then you are doing something wrong, and 3) if people around you are in pain, then you must do something to help them stop the pain.

The Being Model has been called the model of acceptance. Accepting is probably one of the most difficult tasks for those of us brought up and trained in the Doing Model. Accepting pain becomes a herculean challenge. Differentiating between necessary, or acceptable, pain and unnecessary, or unacceptable, pain is difficult and will be dealt with later on. Paradoxically, as soon as we can accept the fact that we cause pain, advertently or inadvertently, then we cause less unnecessary pain. As soon as we can accept that we cannot change the pain of the world, our pain is lessened.

To accept the pain, knowing that you cannot and will not change it, and still to do the best you can, is the task of the hero. To do the best you can, for yourself, for the moment, while simultaneously knowing and feeling pain, without becoming cynical, helpless, or paralyzed by fear of the pain, is also the task of the hero. To put your shoulders back, your eyes up, and to march into a world full of pain without understanding it or needing to explain or justify your innocence is a superheroic task. To be a hero requires Self-Esteem and Social Interest. To have these, one must be able to accept the reality that life involves pain.

Why am I so afraid?

Fear is one of the earliest and most basic emotions. It is necessary for survival of the species and critical for the survival of the infant. The first fear, fear of abandonment, which is inherent in all humans, is realistic as the infant will not survive if abandoned. If the infant or young child is not abandoned and if enough security is provided during the vulnerable childhood, the fear of abandonment will usually diminish. Fear of rejection can be considered to be a component of the fear of abandonment. Almost all fears can be related back to the primary fear of nonlife, or death, which is the outcome of abandonment. Death, fear, abandonment, and rejection are all manifestations of powerlessness or loss of control. We are afraid of what we cannot control.

We are also afraid of what we do not know. How can we control the unknown? Fear is often synonymous with insecurity. How can we feel secure in a world that is out of our control? How can we not be afraid in a world full of pain?

Fear is similar to pain; it is part of life. But the fear of fear can result in a nonlife, the life without risks, explorations, without challenges and without spiritual growth. Fear can produce a vicious circle:

loss of security in the world = fear;
fear = insecurity within;
insecurity within = fear of self;
fear of self = loss of control;
loss of control = paralyzing fear;
paralyzing fear = loss of security in the world.

Being afraid of being afraid can produce the exact outcome that one was trying to avoid by being afraid in the beginning.

Courage is not defined as a lack of fear. Rather, courage means doing something in spite of your fear. It is not courageous to do something that we are not afraid of doing. If we are afraid and still do it, we are doing the hero's task. Paradoxically, the more we do when we are afraid, the less fear we have. And the less we do with our fear, the more power the fear assumes over us.

Being afraid is being human. Being afraid does not mean that you are weak or powerless. Your fear is your feeling; your behavior determines your character. Acknowledge your fear, accept it without criticism, be gentle with yourself because you are afraid, and then do what you have to do anyway. Know that going through the fear is the true act of courage—the way of the hero.

Isn't it "normal" to be insecure, jealous, possessive, depressed, or miserable?

If you define normal as the norm, then the answer to this question would be *yes*! It is normal to see insecurity, envy, arrogance, greed, possessiveness, depression, etc., in almost all of the people that we know. Many of our dysfunctional traits and states are what we commonly call "the human condition." Perhaps it would be more appropriate to call many of our ailments the result of the training in our Model of Doing. Too many of us have been excellent students of an inappropriate and faulty system for coping and living well.

We have been taught that we are our feelings and that we are not responsible for the way that we are feeling. We excuse inappropriate behaviors by saying things like, "Oh well, you know how upset he is" or "It's not her fault because she's having a bad time." We have been trained to believe that our feelings control us, that other people's behaviors control us and that our reactions are not under our own control. How often we hear or say, "You are making me angry" or "What you are doing is making me jealous" or "I can't be angry at them because they can't help themselves" or "The world is making me depressed because nothing is working the way I want it to." There are literally thousands of examples similar to these in which our responsibility for our actions or feelings is given to someone or something outside of our control.

The model of "you are what you do" not only implies that you should be able to control your destiny but that you should also be able to control others around you so that you can achieve your goals. It does not teach us how to control ourselves and it does not teach us what our responsibilities are.

If your goal is to be balanced, to act responsibly, to let go of the craziness of life, to learn Self-Esteem and practice Social Interest, then you will find small comfort in being one of the many miserable people in the world. Misery may love company but how many of us love misery—particularly when it is unnecessary. Unnecessary pain is the pain that results from our own insecurity. Insecurity is not a necessary condition of the human adult. It hampers maturity. Possessiveness, jealousy, and depression, along with a host of other ailments, are not necessary nor do they serve any positive purpose except to confirm what excellent students we have been. There is enough real pain in the world that cannot be conquered. There is no need to make more pain. By learning to be secure with ourselves, we can eliminate the unnecessary pains, the "trauma dramas" of everyday life.

Why can't life be fair?

The reality that life is not fair seems to be one of the most difficult and painful concepts for clients to accept. Perhaps the reason for this is that our western linear model implies that it is a fair world and if you work hard enough and long enough, you will achieve your goals. Perhaps the ideals behind the creation of the United States, the values of equality and fairness for all, have led us to assume that this is the way the world should work. Whatever the reasons, the fact remains that we want the world to be fair. We want to be able to depend on something concrete and we want some guarantees for our safety, security, and well-being. The fact that these guarantees do not exist does not stop us from wanting them. Many of our defense mechanisms, our illusions, and our denials have to do with not accepting the fact that life is unfair.

Life is not fair because "fairness" is a value judgment. This means that what is fair is subjective—it changes according to who is rating what and when and why. What is fair to me today may no longer be fair tomorrow or in different circumstances or around different people. An example: the promotion that I worked hard for but was given to you, is not fair to me but very fair according to your perspective. And even if you agree with me that it was not fair, next month you will justify the fairness of it by believing you are doing a good job.

The importance of the concept that life is not fair is not in the explanation of it but in the acceptance. The question, "Why not?" is a crazy-making one. There will always be reasons why life should be fair to you and you may spend hours defending, denying, fighting, or being depressed because something unfair has happened again. The big issues of unfairness, the life-and-death issues, will never be explained in a way that makes sense. There is no answer to the why question when someone you love is dying. We may know the how—cancer, heart disease, another disease, accident—but we will never know the why. And pondering the why causes dysfunctional behavior. This is a very different process from accepting and grieving. Grief eventually ends; it is a natural process. Wondering why may never end; it is unproductive. At some point, we must let go of the why, accept the reality, and get on with the living.

Trying to make the world fair is both destructive and self-defeating. Many good-natured people run around trying to fix the unfairness of it all. Some of these we call codependents, some are living martyrs, and very few are truly saints. Codependents and living martyrs tend to be filled with anger, resentment, envy, and insecurity. The nonacceptance of this concept creates bitterness, unhappiness, and unnecessary pain and prevents the possibility of growth. This is truly not fair!

The paradox here is that the acceptance of the reality that life is unfair often leads to behaviors which are more objective, more loving and caring, and more realistic than the behaviors of the nonaccepting. These accepting ones are often perceived as more "fair" than those who are trying to force the world to be fair.

What effect does my past have on me?

This can be a very controversial question. Schools of psychology differ dramatically in their treatment of the past and its influence on the individual. Perhaps the simplest answer would be: as much as you *want* or *need* it to have. This answer is recognized as a gross oversimplification in some cases, as the truly traumatic childhood may produce significant blocks to development. In general, however, it is important to realize that no one had the "perfect past" and that all of us have experienced dysfunctional families or homes or educations or friendships.

The major difficulty with the influence of the past on our present mode of living is that the past frequently is credited with responsibility for our present dysfunctional activities and behaviors but all too rarely does the past receive the credit for our superb behaviors and our successes. We like to acknowledge the good stuff as ours right now and blame the bad stuff on the past or someone else.

However, the past is very important to what we are at this moment because it brought us to this place and time. Everything we have done, everything that has happened to us, all of our collective experiences have resulted in exactly who and what we now are. There is absolutely nothing any of us can do to change any part of our past. It is incredible, then, how much energy is wasted on the past—energy that cannot be used productively. If you are spending a significant amount of time living in your past, and you will know so by feeling guilty, by making "what if" and "if only" statements, then you are missing out on your life. You are not living in the present and you are not doing the best you can. You are making the past your enemy and allowing it to steal your time—your life.

Your past, which includes every moment up to this one while you are reading this, is gone. It is over, untouchable, unchangeable. The best way to get out of your past and to let go of any overinfluence it may have on you is again another paradox. Let go by honoring. Stop hating, regretting, fighting, wishing for, and denying. Accept the reality of what you had and what you missed. There is no going back now. Mixed in with all the "shit" (and everyone's past life has large quantities of shit) are some positive things. After all, you have arrived at this place and time. You survived it all. Reward yourself for surviving and honor your past for what it taught you. If you do not like what your past has taught you, honor it anyway for teaching you what does not work. Everything we have learned has value, if for nothing else but to help us prioritize by minimizing our options.

Decide to use your past for your optimum benefit. Take what you need and remember it lovingly. Be objective. Look through your baggage and pick out the good stuff. Let the rest go—from your memory, your actions, your life. Do not be afraid of your past —ask for help in working through it if this task seems overwhelming. You do not need to spend your present and your future life dealing with your past.

What can I do about my future?

We seem to be obsessed with the future. This is understandable when we realize that our Doing Model is a goal-oriented one and that, in this model, nothing is ever enough. No matter what is happening in the present, we have to concentrate on the future. And because, like the past, we cannot live in the future, this orientation takes us out of the present, out of what we can control and manage. Just as guilt lives in the past, anxiety lives in the future. We have become so future-oriented that when we become uncertain about the future, we tend to panic. If the future is shortened by disease or circumstance, we feel cheated and resentful. It seems to be easier to conceive of ourselves as what we *will become* than as what *we are*.

It would be unrealistic for most of us to have no thought for the future. Part of our definition of maturity is taking care of ourselves, both now and later. Therefore, some planning in the here and now needs to be future oriented. We can do things now for tomorrow, hoping that we will have tomorrow and that what we are planning will work later on. The first realization, however, needs to be that our concept of the future is only a concept and not a guarantee. Nothing is certain and no future time is certain. It is unrealistic to think that you can control what will happen to you.

The paradox here is that the more emphasis we have on the present, the more we focus on being the best we can right now, the more the future seems to take care of itself. Once we learn that we cannot control the future—once we give up the illusion of control —fate seems to work in our favor. And if it does not, if calamity occurs, we are better able to accept and deal with it. Because we are survivors, the future is never as bleak or fearful as the fear of the future. Relax. We do not ask this question when we are enjoying the present and feeling secure in ourselves. There is no need for anxiety in the moment. We do not have to panic when we can do something. In the present we can breathe to relax, we can consider our options, we can acknowledge our feelings, we can accept ourselves, we can choose, we can experience, we can be heroes. We can do none of these things in the future. The best we can do in the future is waste the present dreaming about being a hero. Remember, time is not replaceable. Live the moment well, try to stay in the here and now, and there will be no need for anxiety or regret.

🖋 Why don't we need guilt and anxiety?

Both guilt and anxiety are highly self-destructive. Like the Weak Ego, they function to make us feel bad about ourselves. They prevent us from being the best that we are capable of being and they paralyze our actions. They have no viable function in the present. When we are living the moment, we have no time for guilt or anxiety. We are living our lives, rather than judging our lives.

We do not need guilt because we are equipped with a conscience. (In this context, guilt and shame are equivalent.) Our conscience tells us when we have done something wrong. The conscience says things like, "Oops, that was a bad behavior" or "I wish I hadn't done that or said that." Our conscience can be thought of as a gentle teacher, instructing us in the moment how things are progressing and what we need to change. Once you trust yourself, you can trust your conscience.

Guilt, on the other hand, can be thought of as a malevolent dictator. Guilt tells us that we are bad, that the sum of ourselves is inappropriate or evil or uncaring. Guilt takes one action or thought or feeling and generalizes it to the total person. Guilt allows us to feel overwhelmed with negativity and leaves us feeling powerless and helpless. That is why it is such an effective dictator

—it quickly assumes total control over your nature, your behaviors, your life.

Guilt is also insidious in that it perpetuates the continuation of the "bad" behavior. It can be thought of as an evil circle: a snake with its tail in its mouth. This is how guilt generally works: 1) You do something that is unkind or uncaring or destructive to yourself or others, something that you know or feel is wrong, 2) you begin to feel guilty, 3) the guilt grows, 4) you are now feeling acutely and painfully guilty and the pain is overwhelming, 5) you begin to look for a release from all this pain, 6) you start to externalize the reasons for your behavior ("If he did this, then I wouldn't have done that", etc.), 7) you increase the externalizations until you have rationalized and justified your behavior, 8) you believe your justifications, and 9) you repeat the behavior that created the guilt in the first place.

This pattern is well exemplified in the addictive relationship. One partner is the addict, the other is often codependent and the blame for each other's behaviors falls on the other person because of the guilty cycle described above. This addictive thinking goes something like this: I do what I do, I feel bad about it (thereby proving that I am a good person), when the pain becomes unbearable, I transfer the guilt to you thereby justifying my own behaviors and giving me a rationale to continue. This cycle only works in relationships in which we do not take responsibility for ourselves. We need to be responsible. We do not need to feel guilty. Take responsibility for your behaviors. Stop feeling guilty. Next time you feel guilty, stop. Tell yourself that you have done something you do not like. You will learn from this. Next time you will not do the same thing again. Thank your conscience. Reward yourself for taking responsibility. Let go of the guilt.

In the same way, anxiety is not needed. Anxiety can be conceptualized as dreaming something that we do not want to occur. It is worrying about things that have not yet occurred. Once the thing has occurred, we begin to do something about it. How often do we feel a sense of relief when something we have been worrying about actually happens? We can deal with whatever happens in the present; we can never deal directly with anxiety. We don't need it. Anxiety may start out as a bad dream while we are awake but it quickly progresses into a living nightmare. Like guilt, it takes us out of the present and puts us into a painful, discouraging, useless, time-wasting place. Let it go. Live the moment without either guilt or anxiety. We do not need either one when we are living a meaningful life.

Does evil exist?

Yes!!!

Now is the time to present an important paradox: If you are worried about being evil, you most likely are not evil. True evil does not allow for self-doubt or self-examination. (Read M. Scott Peck's book *People of the Lie* for a comprehensive and enlightening discussion of the nature[s] of evil.)

Are evil and being "bad" the same thing? No. We can and will do bad things—inappropriate, uncaring, pain-filled behaviors—because we are human and therefore not perfect. These behaviors do not define us as evil people. This mistake is similar to guilt—overgeneralizing from a behavior to the whole. If we choose to continually commit behaviors which are painful to others and to ourselves, we may become evil. An examination of conscience is required to let us know when to stop, when to change, and when to make amends. If we continue along doing damage to ourselves and to others without questioning our behaviors and if we refuse to acknowledge that we may be doing harm, then we are vulnerable to becoming evil.

The underlying assumption of the theory behind Self-Esteem is that we are good. Lacking a conscience does not mean evil; rather, it means sickness or handicap, in much the same way that lacking a limb means a handicap. The nature of evil implies choice. We cannot choose or be held responsible for choice if we do not have the necessary qualifications for making that choice. Evil can be defined as choosing not to do good. It most often is seen in those who put all their energy into looking "good" and choose not to examine themselves. Evil requires the opposite of Self-Esteem—there can be no exploration of the self, no responsibility for the consequences, and no acceptance of the ability to do wrong (to be human). Interestingly, the externalizations which occur in the circular process of guilt can be conducive to becoming evil. It is easy to imagine an evil person expressing guilt but never changing, doing evil and blaming others. The safest way to avoid evil is to practice Self-Esteem and recognize that we are all imperfect.

Why am I good?

This is essentially a philosophical question which is only asked in therapy after the client begins questioning the Doing Model, their previous training, and the nature of good and evil. Most of us go through life assuming that we are not good and that we need to be punished or controlled or contained as our true natures are base and bad.

One school of thought defines man as essentially bad. From this philosophy evolved the need for power and control, for institutions, such as church and state, to control the masses. These institutions use punishment and strong discipline to keep order, to frighten into submission, and to prevent the spreading of our inherent "badness." This school of thought believes that man cannot make decisions and needs strong leadership (dictatorship) to prevent the crowd from running amok. (William Golding's *Lord of the Flies* is a frightening novel based on this philosophical belief.)

The opposite school of thought chooses to believe that man is inherently good—of God—and that when presented with a choice, prefers to do goodness, even though it may be more difficult and more confusing, over evil.

The paradox of this choice is that while choosing goodness is not the easy choice it does result in an "easier" life. Often the good choice may not feel "right" while the easier choice may feel initially better but may result in a form of evil. A perfect example of this paradox is the concept of caretaking. Our Doing Model defines *all* caretaking behaviors as good. However, a large number of caretaking behaviors are not good. People who are being taken care of cannot feel a sense of mastery or control over their own lives. Therefore, the choice of goodness and the control over this choice belongs to the caretaker rather than the person who is being taken care of, which is the opposite of the intention. A form of evil may exist when the caretaker takes all the credit for the action and does not allow the recipient to have any power or control for the ensuing consequences. In this case, the initial choice not to caretake may be the "good" choice but it will not be the easy one. Making choices involves learning and practice. Practicing your goodness is a trial-and-error process.

You are good! You can choose to practice your goodness. You can assume responsibility for your life and your behaviors. You can take care of yourself. You can believe in your own and in others' goodness. In this way, you can become a role model for goodness.

What is therapy?

There are almost as many definitions of therapy as there are therapists. Therapy is a relationship and, like all relationships, works when both parties are satisfied. There are many schools of therapy, such as the cognitive, behavioral, analytical, humanistic, or gestalt, among others, but in achieving positive results the particular school of therapy does not seem to matter as much as the relationship of the client with the therapist. While it may be helpful, then, to understand what type of therapy you will be getting, the first and most important variable, by far, is that you trust your therapist. There may be times in the therapeutic process in which you are angry or upset with the therapist (this is normal) but at all times trust must be present. The next important variable would be competence. Training and experience are significant variables in this field. Therapists are humans. Humans make mistakes; therefore, therapists can be wrong. Paradoxically, it is easier to trust someone who admits they are wrong than to trust someone who believes they are always right.

Therapy is first and foremost a process. In many ways, it parallels life. The simplest way to think of it is that two people, the therapist and the client, are focusing together on one person's life.

This kind of attention and concentration can be powerful. Often clients will settle for the attention alone, which can be therapeutic. Good therapy needs to be more than attention. There is a strong teaching component to all therapies. Some styles are more directive and some therapists resemble teachers. Other styles are more covert and the teaching is indirect. But teaching, retraining, rethinking, and restructuring need to be included in the change process.

Many clients want their therapists to take charge of their lives. This is *not* what good therapy is about. Neither is therapy about advice giving, problem solving, decision making, although, at times, these components may occur. The therapy will result in a great disservice to the client if it causes the client to become helpless and dependent upon the therapist. The goal of therapy is to help the client become independent. Other goals may deal with maturity, effectiveness, control, and feeling better, but independence—the ability to think and act for oneself—is at the foundation of all therapies.

Self-Esteem therapies seem to share a basis of encouragement of the client. They are similar to other types of supportive therapies in that unconditional acceptance and caring are a critical part of the relationship between the therapist and the client. This does not mean that the therapist likes everything about the client or that every behavior is encouraged. Rather, the therapist will accept the totality of the client and will encourage and reward the attempt at new behaviors.

This book is similar to therapy in that it is trying to teach a new model for living, a new way of looking at yourself, and to offer more choices and options. My two metaphors for therapy are to add more tools to your tool chest, so that on any occasion, you have the right tool for the job, or to add more colors to your palette so that you can expand your repertoire and create more artistically.

Perhaps the most important mission for the therapist is to *en-*

courage! All clients have become dis-couraged in some way about themselves or their lives. It takes courage to do your best in this crazy world. Through en-couragement, the therapist provides a safe place in which to try out new ideas and to use new tools.

Why can't the therapist change (or fix) me?

No one can change anyone else. Period.

You can *only* change yourself. No one else can change you. Other people may think that they are responsible for your change but you are allowing them (overtly or covertly) to think that. Your change is entirely in your control. You choose what you do and what you do not do. You choose which thoughts and feelings to act upon and which to ignore. You choose when to be dependent and when to assert yourself. If you choose to give your personal power to someone else, you are empowering them and you can take back your power whenever you choose.

The word *choose* was deliberately overused in the above paragraph in order to emphasize that your life is in your control. Even when you do not feel in control, you are still the only one giving away your power.

Why does this concept—that we choose and we control our own lives—seem so difficult for so many of us to accept? Probably because originally, as children, we were powerless and unable to choose. Our caretakers had the ultimate power over us—we depended upon them absolutely for our survival. We started our lives feeling helpless and when we did assert ourselves, usually around two years of age, we were called "terrible" and all too frequently punished for not being compliant or "good." Thus, we quickly became afraid of being "bad," which all too often means doing what we want to do.

It is a basic human need to be loved; as infants, we may die without touch and affection even though we are fed and bathed. Our skin needs to be touched, our bodies need to be held, our spirits need to feel loved. We will pay a high price to have these needs filled. Often the price can feel as if we have given ourselves away. We are trained to give our power away and that those who take our power will then give us love in return. Unfortunately, they do not. The paradox here is that people love "whole" people, those with their personal power intact, much more readily than they love helpless, dependent people.

As children and as adolescents, we learn that what we want must be subverted by our more powerful parents, teachers, and peers. When, then, do we learn that it is safe to show our personal power? If we are lucky, we learn it from having healthy relationships or from having wise role models. If we have not found the relationship or the role model, then the therapist can serve this function.

The therapist, or role model, or loving friend, cannot change you. But they can provide an atmosphere and environment conducive to change. And they can en-courage you to assert yourself, to claim your personal power, to take risks, to make mistakes and to know that you are accepted and esteemed at all times.

No one can change you. The opposite is also true. You can change no one except yourself. The therapist will help you to focus your attention on yourself. The time and the energy that you spend on changing yourself will result in you feeling more powerful and more in control of yourself and you will benefit and take credit for what you have done.

What is success?

Our western linear model is a success-oriented model. On this model, success would be defined as the acquisition of things or the achievement of status. Most of us would see a couple dressed in fancy jewelry, custom clothes and shoes, and driving a very expensive car and think that they have achieved success. Most of us believe that success is measured by things and that we can easily see it and covet it. We define people who have reached their goals as successful and people who have not done so as not successful. Education, money, and power seem to be attributes of this definition of success. And the lack of education, money, power, and ambition are the signs of failure. It is important to note that all measures of success on this model are externals to the self. They are all related to the concept of the ego—one's esteem is dependent on other people or things. And because they are externals they are not permanent. How strange to be highly respectable one day and a failure the next because of a stock market crash or a war or a disaster!

There is another problem with this model for success. There are great numbers of people who faithfully follow the formula—study hard, work hard, meet all the "right people" and do all the appropriate things—but they still have not achieved success. Through no fault of their own they have just not "made it." Despite the implicit assumption of the Doing Model—that you can control your destiny—success, as defined above, is not in your control. Luck, fate, and chance all play a big part in determining external success. These are not generally recognized as part of the linear model because there is nothing we can do to control them.

The Being Model does not define success. It is implied that you are successful in your being. Where you are at the moment is your success—you have survived! You are. That is enough. The only way to measure success on this model would be by how you feel about yourself. If you love yourself, especially when the world around you is falling apart, then you are a success. If you do not love yourself, you are not a failure. You just have not learned yet how to love yourself. This definition of success is internal and in your control.

The paradox here is that the far eastern model recognizes and accepts fate, chance, and luck as part of the model and there is no attempt made to control them. They are totally outside of the self and therefore outside of control and all the control is within the person. The person "being," according to this model, has more control, real control, than the person "doing" on the western model, even though the western model presents itself as a model of power and control and success.

You can be a success. You can control how successful you are. You can learn to be successful in the only way that ultimately counts and to the most important person in your life—yourself.

What does God have to do with it?

Everything, if you believe.

Nothing, if you do not.

For the process of learning Self-Esteem, either belief is acceptable. Remember, the circular model is a model of acceptance. We are where we are. We believe what we believe. It is not up to us to believe for others or to convert them to our beliefs.

This theory and my style of therapy began when I doubted the existence of God. I now very strongly believe. For me, God and good are part of the same continuum. Our goodness comes from the God within and we are trying to find the relationship with the God outside of ourselves.

For those who do not believe, please substitute the concept of goodness for God. For those who do not believe in goodness, neither this book nor the concept of Self-Esteem will be meaningful.

What is *the* question?

Once you have decided to be on the circular Being Model and you have chosen to have Self-Esteem, to love yourself and treat yourself in a loving way at all times, then there is only one relevant question. *The* question is:

"How do I feel about myself right now?"

This question needs to be asked often, especially when we are beginning to learn to love ourselves and to practice loving behaviors toward ourselves. This question needs to be asked after thoughts, behaviors, actions, and reactions. It needs to be substituted for "How do they feel about me?" and "What is going on here?" This question will teach you to know yourself, to trust yourself, and to focus your life on exactly what you can control and change.

🐭 What is *the* answer?

This question has two possible answers and two different ways to behave, depending upon your answer to the question "How do I feel about myself right now?"

ANSWER 1: "I feel good about myself. I like what I did or thought or said. I am doing the best that I can."

BEHAVIOR 1: Reward yourself. Pat yourself on the back. Smile at yourself in the mirror. Buy yourself a treat. Say something nice to yourself. Say, "I did well!"

ANSWER 2: "I feel bad. I don't like what I did, said, or thought. I wish I had not done that. I'm uncomfortable about this."

BEHAVIOR 2: Do not punish yourself. Do not say bad things about or to yourself. Do not allow guilt to enter. Simply plan to do something different next time; to try another behavior or thought.

Remember that you need to make mistakes in order to learn. Also remember that by making mistakes and learning from them, you will be expanding your repertoire and practicing utilizing your newly learned skills. You are human—you are imperfect. You will do things that you do not like—do not feel good about. Being human means that you are allowed to make mistakes. Having Self-Esteem means that you can forgive yourself when you make mistakes. Make amends. Be sorry. And then let it go. Get on with living.

II. Conceptual
Issues

What is within my control?

Our western Model of Doing emphasizes control and trains us that power and control are valuable goals. What this model is actually teaching us is the illusion of control. There are only two things in the entire world that are within your control:

1. *The way you choose to feel about yourself.*
2. *Your behaviors, which are based on your own feelings.*

Nothing else is within your control. There is only one exception to the above and that is your young children. You do have some control over their behaviors and you do have control over what you teach them and how they learn to feel about themselves. Once your children have become adolescents, you will quickly, and perhaps painfully, learn how little control you have over them.

If we do not have control over something, then we cannot have total responsibility for it. How often do we take responsibility for others or for consequences that were never within our control to begin with? This concept of control is a critical one for understanding the Being Model and for developing Self-Esteem. As long as we foster an illusion of control and feel responsible for things which are out of our control, we cannot live the reality of our lives and we cannot gain a mastery of ourselves.

It is important to note that number one of the two things above that we can control—the way you feel about yourself—does *not* state "the way you feel" or "your feelings." The way you feel about yourself is a choice and therefore it is within your control. Your feelings are not chosen and not within your control. We carry around with us at all times all of our feelings. We can feel a certain feeling, for example, sadness, without knowing why. The same stimulus from the environment can bring about several feelings or a different feeling can occur in response to the same stimulus at another time. For example, you can be feeling normal while walking across a busy street and almost be hit by a speeding car driven by a stranger. You may now feel angry or sad or resigned, or you may feel a combination of all of these. Or, if you are in a good enough mood, you may not feel anything except lucky that you did not get hit. Your feelings occur spontaneously and they are not in your control.

You can control your choice of how you feel about yourself; you choose whether you love yourself or you choose not to love yourself. Once you have chosen, then your behaviors, referred to in number two, will follow your feeling. If you choose to love yourself, you will choose to behave lovingly toward yourself. You will accept and forgive and act more gently. If you choose not to love yourself, or not to make a choice (which is a choice in itself), then your behaviors will follow your training and you will ignore yourself, criticize and blame, externalize and expect perfection. It is within your control how you treat yourself. Because the world is treating you badly is not an excuse to treat yourself badly.

You cannot control how the world treats you. You can control how you treat the world. Not only can you control your behaviors toward yourself but also you can control your behaviors toward others. Remember, behaviors are not feelings. They are the conscious expression of feelings and they are in your control.

Please note that *controlling others* is missing from the two things in your control. This is not an omission; it is reality.

What is Self-Esteem?

There are many definitions of Self-Esteem and what they all have in common is the concept of esteeming yourself. This translates to loving yourself, respecting yourself, putting yourself first, and meeting your own needs. Self-Esteem is the placement of yourself in very high regard. This means that you not only love yourself but that you *act lovingly* toward yourself at all times. The best and the simplest way to think of having Self-Esteem is to imagine that you love someone very much, that you are always pleased to see them and to talk with them, that spending time with this person is what you most want to be doing, that you think of them lovingly and try to do things to please them. Your beloved is the most important person in the world to you and you will do anything and everything so that they know this. Now put yourself in the role of the beloved and act exactly the same way to yourself. This is Self-Esteem.

Loving yourself and taking care of yourself are the exact opposites of what we have been taught to think and do. We have been trained to esteem others and/or external variables and to measure our self-worth by what we have or by how much we are loved. This is the definition of *Weak Ego:* our worth and esteem are dependent on something outside of ourselves and, therefore, outside our control. When we feel that our esteem is based on having someone else love us, or having the right job, or making enough money, or being "successful," we are putting ourselves at high risk for insecurity and eventual feelings of failure. All things external to self are temporary. They are not ours and we cannot keep them. Therefore, when we entrust our feelings about ourselves to these external variables, when we feel esteemed because we are loved or in the right place at the right time, what happens when things change and we lose our loved ones or our job changes? Our feelings of esteem for ourselves go with the externals that are leaving us. And we are left feeling abandoned and depressed and without worth. This is crazy even though it is the "normal" way of being. Everything changes!! Why risk our esteem to something out of our control?

Remember . . . we can only control our feelings about ourselves and our behaviors based on our feelings. If we choose to love ourselves and to behave lovingly toward ourselves, if we choose to have Self-Esteem, than we have control over ourselves. We do not have to risk losing our own esteem.

The true test of Self-Esteem is to have everything go wrong for us, to have this crazy world turn upside down and to lose all the things we value, and to still love ourselves and to know that we are loved. To treat ourselves in the most gentle, nurturing, loving way when we are in difficulty or pain just as we would treat another person who is hurting—this is having and practicing Self-Esteem.

Why don't I have Self-Esteem naturally?

We probably would have natural Self-Esteem except that it has been rigorously trained out of us by trainers (parents, teachers, friends) who also do not have Self-Esteem. This is because our western model is concerned with power and control and achievement and we have been excellent students for all the concepts of the Weak Ego. We have learned to worry about what others think about us and to try to please those people that we want to influence. We have learned that we ourselves are not as important or as deserving as the people around us. Also, we have been taught that if we love others unselfishly, we will know automatically what they need and that loving others means taking care of their needs. They, supposedly, will be doing the same so that our needs will also be met by those that love us. We have been taught something that simply does not work.

Furthermore, we are not even given the choice of whether we want to learn Self-Esteem versus the model referred to above. At a very early age, we are taught that loving ourselves is selfish and will lead to being conceited and narcissistic and that no one else will want to be around us. Our churches, our parents, our schools are all institutions of control—control over us! All institutions need to have people who believe in them and will follow the rules. The belief that man is not good and needs to be controlled in order to be socialized seems to have led to the fear of allowing individuals to love themselves and to trust that they will be good when left to their own devices. The western model, by training us in the Weak Ego, is a persuasive one in that it seems to offer a manner of being able to control the feelings and behaviors of others by taking care of them and loving them more than we love ourselves. This is just not the case.

If we cannot or choose not to love ourselves, how then can we believe that we are capable of being loved? If all our love and esteem is focused on others, how can we then feel whole and complete and loved within ourselves? And, if we feel bad about ourselves, how can we then be the best we can be? No one can be at their optimum when they feel bad. Finally, if we are following the model and loving others more than we love ourselves and yet we are not getting back from them what we are giving, how can we not feel cheated and resentful? People who feel cheated, abused, and taken advantage of are not the easiest people to love—either for others or for themselves. When we expect others to love us and take care of our needs, we are placing a burden upon them that they cannot fulfill. No one else is going to know exactly what we need at the very moment that we need it! No one else is ever going to be able to love us exactly as we want to be loved! No one else is going to do for us what we can and need to do for ourselves.

Does Self-Esteem mean being selfish?

Literally, yes. But only if selfish is defined as taking care of the self or "self-ish."

The dictionary definition of *selfish* is "being *too much* concerned with one's own welfare." *Too much* has been emphasized because generally we interpret selfish as being *in any way* concerned with one's welfare. Our western model has taught us that selfish is a terrible concept and, in many ways, seems to have confused the idea of being selfish with that of being self-centered. Self-centered is defined as "stationary or unmoving, a center about which other things move; occupied or concerned *only* with one's own affairs; egocentric."

What is the difference between self-ish and self-centered? Self-ish in the Self-Esteem sense involves your relationship with yourself. The self is not the center with others moving around it. No one else is required to perceive the self as the center of anything. Self-ish is a one-man or one-woman show. The focus is simply taking care of your *self*. We can stop trying to be the sun, with others revolving around us, and be content to be stars, shining by ourselves.

No other concept seems to cause as much argument and be so difficult to accept. It would seem that no other concept has been so well ingrained into the very nature of our beings than this idea that it is evil to be selfish. The great paradox here is that the people that we refer to as selfish—the ones that we believe are *too much* concerned with their own welfare, the narcissists of the world—are some of the most insecure and self-centered people around. These people have no Self-Esteem and are unable to take care of their own needs or to love themselves. They spend their time focusing on how to control others and to be the center of their environments. Their energies are on the externals and they are devastated when others finally leave them. These so-called selfish ones are the epitome of Weak Ego and the exact opposite of the self-ish Self-Esteemed ones.

In order to love ourselves, we must know ourselves. In order to fulfill our own needs and wants, we must first know what we need and want. How can we do these things if we do not focus attention on ourselves? Be self-ish. Take care of your precious self. No one else can—not in the way that you want and need.

Can too much Self-Esteem lead to self-centeredness?

No. You cannot have too much Self-Esteem. It is a process and not a goal; not a commodity. It is something that you practice every day. Self-Esteem is a feeling about yourself coupled with behaviors toward yourself. It means being secure and feeling loved and strong and capable. There will be times when you will feel less secure or loved or capable. These are the times when you will become more vulnerable to the "Weak Ego" and you may well want others to put you in the center of their lives and fulfill your needs. Self-centeredness develops when there is not enough Self-Esteem. The best solution to feeling the need for others to take care of you is to give yourself more of what you are wanting others to give. If you need attention, give yourself lots of attention. If you need to hear compliments and to be praised, praise and flatter yourself. Say exactly what you most want to hear. If you do not believe yourself, how can you believe it when others say it?

When we give ourselves exactly what we need, be it praise or gifts or gentle kindnesses, when we feel fulfilled and whole and secure, we then want to be loving toward others. We have more energy to do things for ourselves and for those around us. We are more accepting of the faults of ourselves and of others. Everything seems to become simpler and things seem to work better. We are not upset if people do not do or say what we want because we feel complete.

Perhaps the metaphor of the two cookie jars exemplifies this paradox. We each have two cookie jars inside of us. One is for ourselves and the other is for all the people around us. We have learned to fill the cookie jar for the others and we bake a lot of cookies for this cookie jar. We have been trained not to bake cookies for our own cookie jar and we have also been trained to not even think about doing this for ourselves. Somehow, if we keep on baking cookies for others, our cookie jar will have cookies in it. Supposedly, others will be baking for us and everyone will be happy. But in reality it does not seem to work this way. Our cookie jar is usually empty and if someone does put cookies in it, they are never exactly the kind that we want at that time. No wonder that we start to feel deprived and resentful and angry as we watch others eating the cookies that we have baked. The paradox is so simple: fill your own cookie jar first with exactly what you want and let the overflow go to the other cookie jar. Keep your cookie jar full. Teach your family members to fill their own cookie jars first. Everyone will win.

How can I learn to have Self-Esteem?

The easiest way to learn anything new is to find a good teacher. Teachers of Self-Esteem are not always easy to find. Certainly not all therapists or ministers or counselors are able to teach you how to love yourself. You will need a role model who practices what is being taught—someone who actually knows how to love the self and also knows how to teach this skill. Self-Esteem is a learned skill; very few come by it naturally. Remember, you have learned how *not* to love yourself and now you must relearn how to love yourself.

Think of learning Self-Esteem as you would think of learning any new skill. If you are really determined and you need to do this, you will do it. It is much easier to learn something for the first time before you have learned it incorrectly. For example, you have been studying a foreign language and after several years of study, you discover that your teacher has a terrible accent and has taught you many incorrect pronunciations. In order to speak the language correctly, you must go back and unlearn and replace the wrong with the correct. This is much more difficult than learning it correctly the first time. Much more difficult but not impossible if you are really determined. Self-Esteem is relearning how to think about yourself and how to behave in a loving manner toward yourself. Granted, it would be much easier and more natural to learn the skill of loving yourself as a very young child when the learning is fresh and uncontaminated. Unfortunately, this does not happen to most of us due to the lack of teachers and role models who have Self-Esteem. So we must accept that we were taught by faulty models, through no fault of our own and really no fault of our teachers who were also taught incorrectly. Being angry and resentful that we were not taught Self-Esteem in the past only means that we are wasting time and delaying the acquisition of the skill in the present.

Begin by being determined to learn Self-Esteem. If you want to badly enough, you will. People can learn anything when they are desperate enough. Be desperately determined. Then find some role models—people who clearly have Self-Esteem. These people will not tell you how much they love themselves or how terrific they are. They will show it by their gentle, quiet strength and by their encouraging and reinforcing behaviors toward others. They will look confident and balanced and they will admit and often laugh at their own weaknesses and mistakes. They will not laugh at or judge others but will be more tolerant and accepting of themselves and of others. You will feel good being around these people. It is critical for you to be around those who accept you as you are right now and who encourage you to feel good about yourself.

Once you have found your role models, and these may be a therapist, a teacher, relatives or friends, observe them carefully. How do they handle rejection? Are they trying to be perfect? What do they do when they make mistakes? How do they cope with the many injustices of their lives? Ask them. Watch them. Listen and learn from them. But do not expect them to know all the answers. And do not expect them to carry your pain or to fix you. Good role models are patient and loving teachers whose Self-Esteem is not dependent on you. Good role models are not codependents.

Finally, be prepared to *practice*. And to make mistakes. And to be imperfect. Self-Esteem is a human attribute and a lifelong striving. It is not a quick fix. It is a way of being in the world that allows you to know yourself and to take care of yourself.

Why don't the self-help books work for me?

In the preceding question about how to learn Self-Esteem, reading a self-help book was not mentioned in the answer. This may seem to be a curious omission as this book could be considered a self-help book. There are three reasons why reading a self-help book, even this one, will not lead to the development of Self-Esteem.

The first reason is that most people buy and read these books looking for the quick fix. They are hoping that the book will have the answer and that they will absorb it by reading. Most of the self-help books do have the answers in some form or other but the very nature of Self-Esteem is living it and practicing it and these skills cannot be acquired by simply reading about them. They must be learned by activity and practice. Self-Esteem can only be internalized by practice. It cannot be handed to you and it cannot be acquired by reading about how someone else learned to do it. This does not mean that the self-help books are not valuable. They are, or I would not be writing one, but they are valuable only as a tool to be used. Reading alone will not do it. Reading the books to learn that you are not alone, that others have been where you are and have learned to change and that change is possible helps you to keep at the task. But the books cannot be the cure and most people spend the money and read the books thinking that when they have finished reading, they will magically be different. The books can tell you how to think and what has worked for others but they cannot think for you. No one else can do it for you, not even your chosen role models. You must do this one for yourself.

The second reason most self-help books fail is that they begin with the premise of change. The book is written about how to change yourself, how to do things differently and presumably better than what you are currently doing, how to fix whatever is wrong or broken in your life. This is the same concept that leads one into therapy. What is missing here is the understanding of the concept of acceptance. The paradox here is that in order to change you must first accept yourself. It is very difficult to accept yourself when you are focused on changing yourself. It is much easier to say "I will love myself when . . . I have lost twenty pounds . . . I have that promotion . . . I am loved by someone else . . . I have whatever I need . . . I have changed." Focusing on change is similar to beating your head against a wall trying to get through. Accepting yourself as you are allows you to step back from the wall, observe it without judgment and perhaps to see a doorway in the wall. Acceptance provides the doorway through the wall and allows the change to occur. Acceptance provides the foundation for the change. The very nature of most self-help books is to imply before you begin that you must change in order to accept yourself.

This leads to the third reason why the self-help books fail: the books cannot provide an accepting and encouraging environment. Role models, by accepting you as you are right now, can help you to accept yourself. They can provide the observing eyes to help you look at yourself and find the doorway to change. It has been mentioned that you must do the real work yourself and that learning

Self-Esteem can be a painful process. Your role models can help you to accept yourself and can provide a supportive and facilitative environment for change to occur. The self-help books, including this one, can supplement the learning process. They can best be used as one of several tools but they cannot be the only tool in the learning of Self-Esteem.

If I have Self-Esteem, will I be happy?

Not necessarily. Self-Esteem does not mean happiness. It does mean an awareness of yourself, a deep and lasting respect for yourself and, finally, a great love for yourself. It does not mean that you have control of anything except the way you feel about yourself and your behaviors. Self-Esteem does not mean being able to control your feelings. Happiness is a feeling and therefore not in your control. However, loving yourself often produces a feeling of happiness or great inner contentment. Often, but not always.

Just as you cannot control your feelings, you also cannot control the feelings of others. You really have no control over the behaviors of others and, therefore, you cannot control the environment around you. Since much of our happiness depends on others and the environment, being happy is not usually in our control.

It is important to realize that choosing to love yourself will not change the world but will only change your world. The externals will stay the same but the ways in which you perceive them may be different once you have Self-Esteem. You will be more reluctant to turn your personal power over to things or others that you cannot control. The world will not become fair and bad things will continue to happen, to you and to those you love. Having Self-Esteem will not protect you from feeling the pain of life. It will enable you to cope with this pain. You will still feel sad and fearful and angry and sometimes afraid. But having Self-Esteem means that you will have the strength to trust yourself and to know that you can deal with whatever comes along to the best of your abilities. Loving yourself means that whatever happens, you know that you will be there for yourself. This awareness can make you happy.

Remember, the goal of Self-Esteem is not happiness but inner peace and balance and wholeness. It is unrealistic to live this life, which means coping with pain, and, at the same time, expect to be always happy.

If I have Self-Esteem, will I be perfect?

No, you will never be perfect. The perfect human does not exist. The concept of perfect is a dangerous and destructive illusion. Developing Self-Esteem means becoming aware of and accepting your imperfections. Make peace with what you are and strive to do the best you can but never have perfection as your goal.

When you love yourself you immediately become kinder to yourself. You learn to be gentle with yourself when you make mistakes. You will expect to make mistakes because you are human and you will treat yourself lovingly when you make them. This means that you will stop beating up on yourself for sometimes failing and being wrong and that you will forgive yourself and try something different next time. You will learn to value mistakes as your teachers because you can learn a lot from them. If you were perfect you would no longer need to learn anything new and then how exciting would life be? Self-Esteem means lovingly laughing at your mistakes. It also means taking full responsibility for your actions and choices, whether they have positive or negative results. Most of us do what we do for a reason; Self-Esteem means accepting that sometimes our reasons are faulty.

When you have learned Self-Esteem and you do make mistakes,

which you will, you will be truly sorry for the pain that you have caused, to yourself and to others. It is impossible to live and not cause pain. It is also impossible to die and not cause pain. The Being Model accepts that pain is present and part of life. Self-Esteem means that you stop the pain-blame. This means that you can stop trying to be perfect, accept your imperfect state and your mistakes, and hold realistic expectations for yourself.

Anyway, who *really* wants to be perfect? Think about what that means. How could you relate to anyone else? Who could you understand and who would understand you? How would you know about empathy and sharing? How could you possibly be free of judgments? Imagine how lonely and unreal being perfect would be. Even if you could be perfect, would you really choose to be?

When will I have enough Self-Esteem?

Never. Self-Esteem is not a commodity or a goal. It is a process. You will never say to yourself: "I have arrived. I have enough. I can stop learning and working on myself." These ideas come from our goal-oriented western model and are not reflective of the reality of living. There is no time in your life when you can stop the clock and hold things as they are. Remember the hero's task—to know he cannot change the world but to do his best anyway. Life is a challenge and learning to love yourself is one way to deal with the challenge.

You will really know that you have Self-Esteem when the world around you falls apart, when people you love leave you, when your illusion of security disappears. At this time, you will feel sad, angry, confused, and afraid but you will still love yourself and treat yourself in a loving way. As a matter of fact, this is the time to be more loving to yourself.

You cannot store your Self-Esteem and pull it out when you need it. Practicing Self-Esteem is similar to exercising your body. If you work out every day for a year, and then quit for a month, you will have to begin again. Your body will not retain all the previous workouts and be in the same shape after you have quit. Practicing

Self-Esteem means practicing it all the time. You cannot quit and hope for the same results. You cannot learn to love yourself and then stop and hope that you will feel loved when you need it. But it does get easier the more you practice. After a while, like any habit, it becomes almost second nature to treat yourself well and to ask yourself what you need and want and to then give it to yourself. As in an exercise program, the beginning is always the most difficult because it is unfamiliar. If you practice Self-Esteem every day, after a time you will not be able to imagine going back to the way you were before. And once you experience the feeling of really loving yourself, you will not want to lose it. There will never be enough and you will not think about it in quantitative terms.

How then will I know when I am okay?

Parts of you are okay right now. The only thing to worry about is why you are choosing not to love yourself right now, as you are. As soon as you make the choice to practice Self-Esteem, you will put yourself on the path of being rather than doing. Remember, the Being Model does not judge or compare. You are what you are at the moment. If you want to feel better about yourself, you begin to act in loving ways to yourself. You ask yourself the question, "How do I feel about me right now?" all the time and no matter what your response is, you act lovingly toward yourself. If you feel that you hate yourself, remember you are making a choice. It helps to separate ourselves from our behaviors. It is easier and much less painful to hate our behavior than it is to hate ourself. If you hate your behavior, try to think of something different that you can do next time. Make amends and forgive yourself. Let go.

After a time, you will find that it becomes much easier to choose behaviors that will work in a positive, reinforcing way. You will want to behave in ways that make you feel comfortable about yourself and it will become more difficult to do things which cause you discomfort. It will become second nature to choose behaviors that you like and that enhance your positive feelings about yourself. You will begin to feel more in control of yourself and more proud of yourself and more okay. The entire process becomes a lovely reinforcing circle. You practice loving yourself, you practice loving behaviors, and you find that it becomes easier to love yourself.

How do I accept myself as I am?

This question may be the most important one in this book. The answer lies in learning to accept the reality of ourselves without necessarily agreeing with or liking all the feelings or separate components of what we are accepting. This means that we can agree with or approve of the totality, our wholeness, without agreeing with or approving of all our characteristics. This is the opposite of our training, which implies that we must be perfect before we can accept (agree with and approve of) ourselves. We can begin to accept the reality of ourselves, our totalities, as we are right now without needing to agree with or approve of all our parts, our roles, our behaviors. Acceptance does not mean understanding. Just as most of us will never understand all the complexities of life —war, famine, pain, and death—so we will never understand all the reasons for the complexity of ourselves. Acceptance does not mean change. Our acceptance of life does not change it and our acceptance of ourselves will not change us.

What then is acceptance? It means to take something, to receive willingly, to approve. It may be difficult to approve of ourselves when we are wishing that we were different but it is critical for the development of Self-Esteem to begin to accept the reality and totality of ourselves. Acceptance means seeing ourselves as we are, right now, and allowing ourselves to *be*. As Popeye so wisely stated: "I am what I am and that's all that I am." And it is enough for this moment.

Acceptance of self means really looking at yourself and seeing what you are, inside and out, without judgment. It is the same process as meditating on yourself or being an objective observer of yourself. You suspend the judgment and see what you are all about. You take a good hard look at the reality of yourself. This process is not easy but it is necessary. One way to do this is to stand naked in front of a mirror and look at yourself. Do not stop looking when you see something you do not like. Keep looking until you become neutral about what you are seeing. Now you have observing eyes. Keep looking at yourself until you see past the skin and the fat and the surface. Keep looking until you can see through the externals. Do not be afraid. You are observing the reality of yourself. And when you have seen it all, accept it. This is you, warts and all. You will see some good things, external and internal, that you want to keep and you will see some things that you want to get rid of. You will see a human being. Do not act or react. Merely observe. And when you are finished, tell yourself that everything you have seen is okay. Not good or bad, right or wrong, but just okay. This is acceptance.

Another way to learn to accept yourself is to take a piece of paper and draw a vertical line down the middle. On one side label the column "Things I like about me." Label the other side "Things I don't like about me." Then fill in both columns. Take your time and add things as they occur to you. Again, do not be afraid. Most people find it easier to fill in the "don't like" side and they have more difficulty with the "like side." This is because of our faulty training. Keep at it until you have a composite picture of yourself. If you need help, ask your family and friends and especially your role models for help. When you have finished, think about a coin.

A coin has two sides. Neither side is right or wrong or better. Now think of your lists as two sides of the coin. In order to have one side, you must have the other. Try to figure out how the one side depends on the other. For example, if you like the fact that you are an organized person and you dislike the fact that you are too compulsive over certain things, try to see the relationship between the two. You cannot always be organized without sometimes being compulsive. If you like the fact that you are patient and dislike the fact that you are sometimes slow and pedantic, again see the relationship between the two. You may really like the fact that you are a generous person, financially and emotionally, but you may dislike the fact that you sometimes feel that others take advantage of you. Can you see the relationship between the two sides—the light side and the dark side—the side we like and show to others and the side we dislike and try to keep hidden?

Nearly everything that you do not like has an opposite in something that you do like. If you need help finding the positive side to something negative, ask for help. Remember that you cannot be perfect and also remember to suspend judgment. Just as you cannot be perfect, you also cannot be a perfect failure. Everything that you do not like about yourself has a counterpart in something positive. Stop looking only at the negatives and accept the positives. Try to find the balance between the two.

Acceptance is the beginning. It allows change to occur. You do not have to change in order to accept yourself. Your role models will see the positives in you. Your role models, by seeing the good in you, will give you permission to see the good in yourself. Do not be afraid; the good is there.

How can I accept myself if I don't agree with or understand myself?

Accepting yourself involves both behavioral and thought processes. As mentioned in the previous question, there are behavioral techniques you can use to begin the process. The cognitive processes toward acceptance of yourself begin when you do the following:

1) Stop the denial. Stop thinking that you cannot accept yourself. You can and you will if you really want to.

2) Suspend the judgment. Not everything in the world can be viewed in terms of dichotomies. Not everything is good or bad, right or wrong, positive or negative.

3) Recognize your defenses. They are stopping you from movement. They may have worked in the past but now they are in the way.

4) Kill your illusions. Reality is not illusory. Reality is and the reality of yourself exists. Everyone else around you knows the reality of you. Now it is time for you to know yourself.

5) Utilize conscious, reflective observation. Observe yourself

as others observe you. To others, you are what you do and not what you wish that you were doing. Your behaviors do count and you can control them. Your feelings, your dreams, your hopes, and your wishes are not the reality of you. They are only a part of what you are.

There are many things that we accept but do not agree with or understand. War, famine, the unfairness of life, and death are things that we deal with every day. We accept that these things exist even though we may not like them and clearly we do not completely understand them. We are part of all of it and our very existence is proof that we are living something that we do not fully comprehend. You may not like your life, you may not like yourself, you may wish to be someone or somewhere else. Your feelings will not change the reality of your situation. Your behaviors will change you. Acceptance of self becomes a behavior. You can do it.

Acceptance is not giving up or giving in. It takes less work and less energy to accept yourself than it does to deny yourself. In the long run, it is a much easier process and you will find that acceptance frees up the energy needed to have Self-Esteem and to do the best you can. It is only in the beginning that it seems difficult and strange. Remember, you are relearning a skill. This takes time and feels "wrong." Keep at it. Stay with it. Acceptance really works. Everything after acceptance is easier. But if you cannot accept yourself, you cannot know yourself. And if you do not know yourself, you will never believe and trust that you love yourself. And that you are truly lovable. Accept that you are lovable. You are good and you are worthy of love. Believe this and self-love, Self-Esteem, will be yours.

How do I begin to love myself and take care of myself?

You "fall in love" with yourself in much the same way that you fall in love with another. First, you notice yourself and you pay attention to the little things that you do—the things you say and the way you say them, the way you move, the way you laugh, the things you like and don't like, and so on. You accept yourself in the same way that you would accept someone else that you are interested in. You forgive yourself for your mistakes and you compliment yourself for your achievements. You are nice to yourself and you make allowances when things go wrong. You notice and take credit for the accomplishments. You give yourself compliments and say the same kinds of things to yourself that you would say to your beloved. You take time out for yourself when you are needy and you treat yourself gently when you are hurt. You smile at yourself in the mirror and you tell yourself "I love you" every day. It may feel silly or awkward at first but you do it anyway. Do you remember the first time you told someone that you loved them? How nervous you were and how afraid of rejection or commitment? This is usually what happens the first time that you look in the mirror and say "I love you" to yourself. It is simple but it is not easy. Try it and accept whatever happens. As in a relationship, it takes a while before we really believe it. But if you keep saying it often enough you will eventually believe it.

Telling yourself is not enough, just as it is not enough to just tell someone else. You must behave in a loving way to yourself and you must do this consistently and frequently. Just as no one else would believe that you really loved them if you only told them you did and then proceeded to ignore them or berate them or treat them badly (at least, no healthy person would believe they were loved under these conditions), you yourself will not learn to believe that you love yourself unless your behaviors match your words. It is important to say to yourself "I love you" because we need to hear these words but it is equally important to act lovingly toward yourself most of the time. (Most rather than all because we are not perfect and sometimes we forget.) By the way, saying "I like you" is *not* the same thing at all as saying "I love you." If you have ever loved someone who liked you back, then you will understand the qualitative difference. Self-Esteem means loving yourself even when you don't always like yourself.

When given this assignment to look in the mirror and say "I love you" and to behave lovingly toward themselves, most people express great frustration because they do not *feel* loved or loving. If this occurs to you, know that this is normal. Keep at it. The feeling of love will follow the behaviors of loving. One day you will look in the mirror and you will feel loved. Remember, love is a verb and a verb describes activity. Loving yourself is something you do and when you do it enough, you will feel it. The behavior is in your control; the feeling is not.

You take care of yourself in the same manner in which you take care of another. First, you ask yourself what you want. If you do not know, then ask yourself what you need. If your answer is realistic or possible, give it to yourself. If your answer is neither realistic nor possible, find a substitute that is and give that to yourself. Always give yourself something. Remember when you were a child and wanted something unattainable, how quickly you were satisfied with a substitute? Only when nothing was given did you feel cheated or unloved. Be generous and give lovingly to yourself. Act *as if* you love yourself; soon you will.

What is wrong with having illusions?

As mentioned, it is necessary to kill our illusions in order to learn acceptance. Why? Illusions, expectations, myths, and wishes are necessary precursors to the unexplored life. They are often used to prevent the reality of life from causing pain. They frequently serve to keep us from living the moment. They may seem innocuous but they often prevent us from experiencing our lives, our feelings—pleasant and painful. We tend to use them to buffer, to defend, and to change the moment. When utilized in this manner, their cost is too high. They may well keep out the pain, but while doing so they also anesthetize us from living. When we use illusions to defend us from pain, we are using them as drugs; we are no longer wide awake, alert, responsible, and aware of ourselves in the moment. We are no longer in control of ourselves.

By definition, illusions are fantasies. They do not represent the reality of our lives. They frequently represent unattainable goals. They waste our valuable time and they stop us from getting down to the real business of living. If we spend our lives fantasizing about what we want but do not have, we have less time to enjoy what we do have. Our western model does not teach us to enjoy the moment. Instead, we are trained to be focused on where we have been (the past) or where we are going (the future). There is no place in the here and now for illusions.

Just as we must accept ourselves in order to know ourselves, so must we explore ourselves. And this exploration must be real. The unexplored life is not living; it is dreaming. In order to learn about life and about ourselves within this life, we need to be willing to explore. Illusions are easy. Expectations are killers. Neither helps to deal with the moment and both frequently tend to cause problems when we are forced to confront the reality of our lives. If we have the illusion that everything will be better when X occurs, then we will have little incentive to go out and change our lives. Instead, we will sit around and passively wait for X to occur or we focus all our energies into forcing X to occur and if it does occur, we frequently find that we are no better off than before. In fact, we may feel much worse; we may become frustrated and depressed. Illusions tend to produce passive behaviors or the unrealistic need to control things that are out of our control. They are a means to externalize and therefore avoid the reality of the situation. They mean that we are spending the moment living in the future—in the never-never land of "What if?" Expectations are similar in that they indicate that we are living in the future. Expectations mean imagining something, either good or bad, that is not in our control. The time we spend imagining is time wasted. We can do nothing about the future except live it when it becomes the present. We can do a lot of things in the present, but not if we are dreaming or expecting the future.

Illusions can be fun if we do not take them seriously. Dreaming, hoping, and planning can be constructive tasks if they are based on the reality of the moment. Future visions can be productive when they are realistic and attainable. If you know that you are moving to a new city in six months, you can dream about what your life will be like and you will plan for the move. These are normal events and reality based. The danger begins when your illusions transcend the reality and you begin to dream that everything will change because, and only because, you have moved. You are now creating a set of expectations that can only lead to failure. Remember, you take yourself with you wherever you go. And you take any unresolved problems with you. If you use illusions and expectations, dreams and wishes as an escape from yourself and your life, you will quickly find that they will not work. You cannot escape yourself. It is much simpler to deal with yourself, here and now, in this moment and to let go of the illusions. The reality can be enough. Life is worth living and life is now. Having future goals and visions, and working toward them, can give extra meaning to the present if, and only if, your Self-Esteem is not based on your future success.

There may be times when the present is too painful and the only hope is that there will be less pain in the future. Knowing that the pain will pass is not an illusion. Recognizing that change will occur and that change will produce a better situation is called hope. What we do and how we handle the painful present is active behavior. Riding through the pain is quite different from denying it. Allowing the pain to exist, accepting yourself as being in pain, remembering that this pain will decrease over time and that you will be stronger for having experienced your pain are entirely different processes than utilizing illusions to deny the pain. The explored life recognizes that pain is part of the reality of life. Illusions, dreams, expectations, and wishes stop this exploration process. That is why they are dangerous.

Why can't I keep my defenses?

We all have defenses. They are used to protect us from what we cannot handle. Just as the body will go into shock when it suffers a trauma, in order to protect itself from too much pain, so will defenses occur when the emotional pain is overwhelming. Just as shock can only protect the physical body for a temporary period and then the shock itself becomes dangerous and often fatal, so the overuse of defenses also can become emotionally fatal. Dependence on our defenses can be addictive, and like all addictions, can stop us from experiencing the reality of our lives.

What are our defenses? Denial, repression, externalization, rationalization, and intellectualization are some of the more familiar ones. They allow us to explain behaviors that we do not want to deal with. They help us to produce a facade for ourselves and for others when we do not want to see things or accept things as they really are. They tend to cover life and to excuse the unpleasantness of our behaviors and our thoughts and our feelings. We use them when we do not want to deal with our imperfections and those of people we care about. We use them to avoid the fact that life is painful, that death is present, and that we all have a dark side which we do not like. We become defensive when we have to admit that we are not perfect, that life is not fair, and when we are feeling weak and helpless. And the more we use them, the more we need them. As with any drug, they soon take over and we may discover that we cannot operate without them. They become unconscious habits.

What is the antidote? How can we stop using defenses that we are not always conscious of having? First, take responsibility for yourself: Accept that you are human and cannot be perfect. You make mistakes and you have a dark side, a shadow self. Sometimes you do bad things, stupid things, and painful things. We all do. One of the great ironies of life is that the people who know us best know our dark side and see past the facade. Another irony is that once we admit to our secret shadow side, it loses most of its power over us. Being responsible for yourself is one way to admit that you are aware of your faults.

Because the defenses operate to avoid the pain of reality, the second way to stop needing them is to accept the pain. You cannot deny or repress or rationalize something that you admit to and accept. Acceptance produces the necessary strength to ride through the pain. It takes much less energy to admit that you are in pain and to deal with the pain than it does to deny or intellectualize what you are feeling. It is not weakness to feel pain; it is human.

Once you take responsibility for yourself and admit that you feel pain, you will free yourself from the need for your defenses. Defense mechanisms only work well when we are not consciously aware of them. Taking responsibility for yourself, for your behaviors, means that you no longer need to defend against yourself. Admitting your weaknesses and accepting your humanness allows you to let your defenses go. You no longer need them to protect you. You will become strong enough to deal with your pain. Becoming aware of what you are doing and when you are defending yourself is part of having Self-Esteem. And Self-Esteem means letting go, not keeping, the things that stop us from knowing ourselves, such as our defenses.

How can I learn to let go?

Previous questions have emphasized the importance of letting go. It has been mentioned that we need to let go of insecurity, guilt, anxiety, perfection, fairness, and our illusions and defenses. This sounds like a great deal to release and if we do manage to let go of all the above, what will be left?

It is important to note that all of these attributes are related to the Weak Ego, the worth that we receive from external sources. All of the above serve to protect us from ourselves and to provide reasons to externalize or excuse our human behaviors. They all help to justify why we are the way we are and to prevent us from taking responsibility and from changing ourselves.

When we let go of the need to be something we cannot be— perfect—we will discover that what we have left is our humanness, our goodness, our belief and trust in ourselves. We will be left with a kind, objective, and responsible self. We will be left also with the realization that we make mistakes, feel pain, and often do not know why. What is wrong with that?

The best way to learn to let go of anything is lovingly. Do not hate or fight what you are trying to let go of. Rather, honor all of it and realize that all of these things, your past, your guilt, your defenses and illusions, brought you to this place where you are right now. All of these things made you what you are and all of them worked for you because you survived. Think of all these things as tools, albeit faulty tools, but tools nonetheless because they got you here. And now you need new tools, better tools, to get you where you want to be. Respect the old tools before you throw them away, before you let go.

It is always much easier to let go of something that we have outgrown than it is to let go of something we hate or are angry with. When we hate something and try to get rid of it, it tends to become sticky and to cling to us. When we lovingly let go and see the value of what we are getting rid of, it tends to slide away more easily. A good example of this is a relationship that you have outgrown. If you can focus on the good things in the relationship and what you learned from it, the leaving is easier and you tend to feel okay about yourself. But if you can only focus on the hatred and the negativity, the relationship still exerts power over you and you are not free and not feeling okay about yourself.

Honor all of the things that you want to let go of. Look on each of them and remember how they worked for you. Appreciate them for getting you here. Tell yourself that now that you are strong enough and responsible to yourself, you no longer need what you once needed. All of development means letting go and moving on. When we need a crutch, it is nice to have one handy. When we no longer need it, we can gently and lovingly put it away. The more Self-Esteem you develop, the more crutches you will put away. The crutch only becomes an impediment when you no longer need it. Letting go is a process. It takes time. It is an easier process when done with love.

How do I get over my past?

Letting go of our past may seem impossible. How can we let go of something that is so much a part of us? And why let the past go? Aren't we what we are because of our past lives? The answer to this last question is the reason why we need to let go of the past. Yes, to a great extent, we are what we are because of what happened to us in the past. But we are more than that—we can only be who we are right now in the present. Clinging to the past in order to affirm or to excuse ourselves in the present is as dangerous as living in future illusions. Neither one is the reality of ourselves. Neither one is in our control.

Letting go of our past does not mean forgetting our past. Memories are part of us but they are not the reality of who we are right now. The now we can choose; the past we could not. In other words, we cannot be held responsible for things that we could not control. And we cannot control our past. It is done. We cannot go back and do it again. That is why it is important to let go and move on.

Nothing seems to keep us more stuck than hauling the past around with us. It may help to think of our past as a huge garbage bag full of good and bad things. Carrying around this bag only weighs us down and impedes our present movement. We cannot function to our best capacities when carrying around a heavy bag. Put the bag down, open it and carefully go through the contents. Try to separate what was good and what was valued from what was bad and what you hate. Use your objective eyes and you will see that often something that was perceived as "bad" had beneficial results while something that was initially valued as "good" may have produced negative results. Honor all of your past. All of it got you here. Take what you still really need and lovingly let the rest go. You do not need to carry it all around with you anymore. It may help to think of your past as a coat that you once wore as a child. At the time, the coat fit you and it kept you warm. It served its purpose. Now you have outgrown the coat and it will not keep you warm. Why are you still carrying this coat around?

Mentioned above is the fact that you cannot go back and change the past. But you can change the influence that your past has on you right now, in the present. To do this, you must stop trying to make the past something it was not. If you were abused or rejected or unloved in the past, you can stop being abused, rejected, and unloved now. Only if you are stuck in the past will you continue to repeat the patterns of your past. To be free of these patterns, you must let go. Loving yourself when you have not felt loved in your past may be difficult but it can be done. If you choose to let your past write the script for your present life, then you must take responsibility for that choice. It is your life and you are more than what you have been before. Be the best you can be. Let go of what is holding you back. Be free. The past may feel like a prison, but you do have the key and you can walk away whenever you choose to let go.

Perhaps the most effective way to let go of the past is to become aware of the inner child and to learn to parent this child. These concepts will be discussed in the following two questions and answers.

Who is this inner child?

Emotionally we never "grow up." Our feelings do not mature. Anger or sadness in a two-year-old are the same emotions in an adult. The way in which we express our feelings can be immature or mature manifestations of the emotions but the feelings themselves are timeless.

One way to think of the inner child is as the unappointed guardian of our emotional warehouse. He or she rules over our emotions and our needs until the needs are met and the emotions are acknowledged. Only when the inner child is parented (taken care of) will she or he allow the adult side of ourselves to guard the warehouse. What is stored in this warehouse which is the domain of the inner child? All the pain, all the rejections, the loneliness, the abandonment, the fears and insecurities of our lives. Every time we have been hurt, every rejection, every painful message that we have ever received is stored away in the inner child. How do we know that our inner child is there? Every time that we overreact to a stimulus, the inner child is acting out. Whenever we feel out of control and helpless, our inner child has taken over. Whenever our needs are controlling our behaviors, the inner child is demanding to be taken care of. Each time that we feel helpless or hopeless or completely overwhelmed, and the feelings do not match the reality of the situation, our inner child is yelling for attention.

Does everyone have an inner child? Yes. All of us began by perceiving the world through the child's eyes. And all of us have some memories of those perceptions. The child within us remembers the helplessness of feeling out of control. This child has countless experiences of unfairness and he or she remembers all of them. This child personally knows how difficult it is to make sense of a world which is incomprehensible. The inner child has learned what works in the short-term and what works is to yell and scream and demand attention or to become passive, withdrawn, and helpless and to wait for help. If help does not arrive, then hopelessness sets in. Whether the child overtly acts out or passively withdraws, the inner child knows that he or she does not have control over what will happen. A healthy inner child knows how to trust that his or her needs will be met and this child learns how to delay gratification. Most of us, unfortunately, do not have healthy inner children.

Most of us are aware that we have several roles or facets of ourselves: the adult side, the child side, the parent side, the professional side, and so on. As adults, we tend to like the grown-up sides of ourselves and to deny or ignore the childish sides, especially when we are embarrassed by the behaviors exhibited by the child. Most of us are trained to feel that we should be "grown up" and we tend to suppress our child. We certainly suppress the negative side of the child, the acting-out side, but we also suppress the positive side, the spontaneous, excited, playful side. Our inner child will only be suppressed temporarily. The child will come out when we are least expecting it and he or she will often behave in a shocking way. It is as if this child is trying to get back at us for not giving the attention she or he needs. Most of us are in a power struggle with our inner child. What we do not realize is that the inner child has control of our emotions while we try to control our logical thoughts. And we know, perhaps too painfully, that emotions usually rule over logic. The inner child is powerful only when not recognized and when the pain is not acknowledged. This is the secret of the inner child.

What can I do for my inner child?

Begin by recognizing your inner child. Then acknowledge that your child is in pain even if you do not understand all of the pain. Remember what it feels like to be a child in pain. Allow your inner child to be angry with you. Know that you are more than your inner child and that you are the only one who can take care of your child.

How do you recognize your inner child? It helps to go through old photo albums, if available, and to find a picture of yourself before you were five years old. Take the picture out and put it somewhere where you will look at it often. If you can, carry it around with you and look at it several times each day. Become familiar with the way your inner child looks; it is more difficult to deny or ignore someone that we see every day. Try to remember what life was really like for this child. And how the child felt during its childhood. Go back into your past with your child's eyes. Remember, you are not your child and you will not get stuck in your past as your inner child is. You must know what you are dealing with before you can help your child. Next time that you overreact to something, or feel helpless or out of control, think of your inner child as trying to communicate with you. Your child can only get your attention by using strong emotions. Do not be angry at yourself (i.e., your inner child) when you experience these strong emotions. Your anger only causes the inner child more pain and pain is what the inner child is yelling about.

Acknowledge that your inner child is in pain even if you do not understand all of it. Your inner child is angry, sad, and afraid, all at the same time, and many of these feelings are directed at you. The child is angry and sad that you, the only person who can help, are ignoring him or her. Your inner child is afraid that you will never help, that you will never rescue and love and parent in the way that she or he needs. Remember that your inner child is only a little child, without the skills and resources that you have, and that this small child is carrying far too much pain and confusion for any child to deal with.

Separate yourself from your inner child. You are the adult, the parent, the wise one, and you have the necessary skills to parent the child. Do not be afraid of your child. Remember that your inner child is only powerful when you deny and ignore this child. All that is wanted is what every child wants—to be loved and protected and safe. You, and you alone, can give your child what is needed. This may be a good time for you to ask for help. Many therapists are familiar with the concept of the inner child and can help you parent your child. There are several excellent books on this topic which can help you learn to parent your child. You can also learn by observing; if you are a reasonably competent parent yourself (no parent is perfect!), pay attention to what you do with your own children. If you are not a parent, observe someone who is. What do they do when their child is hurt? needs assurance? acts out? What do they say to calm the child? How do they communicate love to their child?

Begin to talk to your child. Say things like, "I am here. I hear you. I know that you are upset. I want to help. You don't have to worry, I'll take care of you. I am not angry with you. I understand.

Everything will be all right. You are good. I love you." Do not expect the child to trust you immediately. He or she has been waiting a long time for you and may need to test you before trusting you. This testing may result in an increase in the behaviors that you do not like. You may find yourself feeling out of control and overreacting more frequently than before. Or you may think that the inner child is not there because he or she seems so passive and withdrawn. Stay with the gentle parenting behaviors. Your inner child is paying attention. Prepare yourself to become the "ideal parent," the parent that your inner child never had but always wanted. No matter how wonderful your actual parents may have been, no matter how much attention they gave you and how much love they showered on you, it could never be enough for your inner child. You have one big advantage over your actual parents: because your inner child is part of you, you will know exactly what your child needs, when it needs it, and you will be able to fulfill all of its needs. You are the ideal parent for your child and your inner child is the only one for which you can be ideal. There is no such thing as perfect but this relationship between you and your inner child is the closest to a perfect relationship that you will ever have.

It is not enough to recognize and accept your inner child. In order for your inner child to heal, he or she must be loved and since you are the only person that matters to the inner child, you must love him or her. In order to learn to love this inner child that has created problems for you, that has acted out and embarrassed you so many times, that has left you feeling helpless and weak and immature, in order to learn to love this "little monster" inside of you, you must stop being angry, stop criticizing, blaming, and punishing this child. Accept your inner child, pay attention to him or her when the child needs your attention. You cannot do this on your time; you must attend to the child on his or her time. Understand that your child is angry with you but that this anger will go away. Recognize that it is not your fault that the inner child is hurt. You did not cause all the pain and you could not alleviate the pain until now. Do not be hard on yourself or the child will think that you are being hard on him or her. Know that children always internalize the pain around them. They think it is their fault and that they are responsible. They try to be good so that the situation will improve, and when it does not improve, they blame themselves. The inner child will think that it is his or her fault if you become a frustrated parent or if you give up.

Good parenting does not mean giving in to the child. When your inner child is acting out, you can help control him or her by structure and loving discipline. You can teach your inner child to learn to delay gratification as long as the child knows that gratification will occur. If you become aware of your inner child demanding attention, and you are not in a situation to stop everything and attend to this child, you can say to your inner child: "I hear you. I know you are upset. We will deal with this soon. Let me do what I must do right now and then I'll attend to you." This is not denying the inner child because you are aware of the message he or she is sending. This is helping the inner child to know that you are in control and that you will take care of him or her as soon as possible. It is critical to keep your promise and to attend to the child or she or he will not trust you next time. Be a loving and firm parent; the inner child needs structure and control.

The simplest way to learn to love your inner child is to do all the things that you have learned in order to love yourself. In other words, follow the behaviors for developing Self-Esteem for yourself with your inner child as well as with yourself. You can learn to love yourself and your inner child at the same time. Loving your inner child allows you to love yourself. If you cannot or choose not to love your inner child, you will not be able to have Self-Esteem. The unloved inner child will still remain the guardian of your emotional warehouse and you will be at war with yourself.

When you choose to love your inner child, what will happen?

Several things, and all of them wonderful. Your inner child will begin to feel safe and protected and will stop being angry and needy. The inner child will stop being your emotional guardian and will let you be in charge of the warehouse. You will no longer have unexpected outbursts from your child and you will truly be in control of your behaviors. Your inner child will let go and allow you to function as an adult. Your inner child will become what it really is—just a small child inside of you—and you will become a more powerful and loving adult. Your inner child will know that when he or she needs attention, he or she does not have to act out, only to ask, and you will attend to him or her. Small children really need very little to be happy. And best of all, your loved and happy inner child will allow you to be a loved and happy and, at times, spontaneous and playful, childish adult. It is very difficult for an adult to function at their best when they are carrying a screaming two-year-old around with them. But think how much joy and love you have for that same two-year-old when she or he is content and smiling lovingly up at you. Your inner child deserves to be loved, as you do. Learn self-love for both of you. The only thing you will lose is the pain of your past.

How can I stop the pain?

As just mentioned, parenting your inner child will stop the pain of the past. But what about your present pain, the pain that you are experiencing right now?

Pain that works for us, natural pain, always has an end. It is part of the healthy physical and emotional body to strive toward the condition of no pain. There are physical illnesses and afflictions which cause chronic pain. Fortunately, emotional pain does not have to become chronic unless we work at it by holding on to the pain. The natural process of pain, with some physical exceptions, is that it will abate over time. Acceptance of the pain and awareness of the pain while it is occurring, called "riding the pain," also help to alleviate the pain as quickly as possible.

There is always a reason for natural pain. Something has happened to you, something traumatic, and it hurts. Emotional pain is frequently caused by loss and when we lose something, it is normal to feel the pain of that loss. To lose something we value and not be in pain is an abnormal response, meaning that we either did not really value what we lost and therefore we are not in pain or that we are denying what we are feeling or that we are incapable of feeling. Feeling the pain, as much as we may not want to, is far preferable to denying or repressing it because, at some time, we will have to deal with the pain and it will be worse later on than it is now. Not being able to feel pain is not a healthy response and people who are this blunted are usually emotionally ill. Pain is a great equalizer. All humans know pain because it is part of the process of living.

Pain is a great teacher. It teaches us patience, and humility and empathy toward others. It teaches us that we are alive and it puts life in perspective. When we are in real pain, we know how unimportant are most of the things that we worry and fret about. We can learn to value the times that we are not in pain. Even so, most of us would prefer not to be in pain and we will expend a great deal of energy trying to avoid it. Some people, however, get hooked on pain. They use it to get attention, to have their needs met, to feel less lonely, and to feel more alive. This pain is what I call unnatural pain. Long after it would naturally abate, the pain is still there and it is being used for secondary gains. This can become a very sick process and pain addicts need professional help in order to let go of their pain.

If your pain is realistic and a normal response to the reality of your situation, you can minimize this pain by doing the following: Accept it and know it will pass. Stop fighting it and honor it as much as you can. Stop hating it. Do not be angry with yourself because you are in pain. Treat yourself even more gently and lovingly than usual. Let others help. Most people can relate to your pain because they have felt pain too. It is not important why you are feeling pain when you ask for help because we can share the pain without sharing the cause of it. Do not be afraid of your pain. You can deal with what you are feeling if you allow your body to know its limits. We have incredible physical and emotional pain-relieving resources programmed into ourselves. Allow them to operate. Know that the pain will pass and that when it is at its worst and you cannot stand it, it will begin to abate. Pay attention to the pain-free moments and you will notice that they increase every day. Use the pain to prioritize your life. Pay attention to the things that really matter. Finally, recognize that riding through your pain will make you stronger, more caring, more empathetic and accepting of others and more loving.

Why must I go through more pain?

Change is painful. Any new learning involves some pain. Relearning involves even more. Pain is a normal component of growth and evolution. Remember the "growing pains" when you were young?

Learning to love yourself, to have Self-Esteem, means turning away from a model that you are familiar with and working with a new model that looks and feels awkward and strange. This is painful. Anything familiar, even though it may cause pain itself, feels like a loss when you initially turn away from it. Think about terrible relationships that you have known or perhaps been involved in. Often the only reason that people give for staying in the destructive relationship is that it is familiar—comfortably uncomfortable. Somehow the unknown, merely by virtue of being unfamiliar, is more frightening than the pain-filled known. This may seem a little crazy but it occurs frequently. Our western model has taught us not to take emotional risks and to set our goals and to achieve them or we are failures. This leaves us choosing to experience terrible pain rather than to admit to being failures—unable to meet the preset goals, like making a bad relationship work.

The truth about pain is that we have to go through it no matter what we do. Therefore, using the pain as an excuse not to try something new, like learning Self-Esteem, will not work because we will not avoid the pain by refusing to change. We are changing all the time. Life is not static and people are not fixed. All development requires change and change is initially painful.

The secret to dealing with future pain is to know that it will occur and to stop being afraid of it. If you are not experiencing pain in the present, why are you worrying now about something inevitable and not in your control? Rejoice in the fact that you are currently pain free and trust yourself that you will be able to deal with your future pain when it occurs. Being afraid of the pain of life has stopped many from living their lives to the fullest. If you are one of the fearful ones, think about the definition of courage. Courage means to be afraid and to do it anyway. If you are not afraid while you are doing something, then you are not being courageous. It takes more guts to go out and live when you are afraid of the pain of life than it does to live without fear. Begin by being courageous and live your life in spite of your fear of the pain. After a short while, your new behaviors will become familiar and you will no longer be afraid of the future pain of living. And when pain does occur, and it will, you will be able to cope with it and let it go.

Is there a relationship between pain, Self-Esteem, and exercise?

Yes. Exercise, any type of physical activity, enhances the good feelings about ourselves and also helps to alleviate our pain. It is much more difficult to feel terrible about yourself when you are moving about or doing an activity. It becomes much more difficult to focus on our negative feelings, our depression, and our emotional pain when we are interacting with our environment. Research has shown that walking energetically with your head held high is an antidote for depression. Being aware of your environment and feeling a part of it helps to take the focus off of yourself and your negative feelings.

However, there is a difference between purposeful activity, such as exercising, and frantic activity in which you are moving around aimlessly. When we are doing the latter, we are trying to escape from ourselves and we waste a lot of energy and time. We are on a treadmill, moving around but going nowhere. When we are exercising, we are in control of our bodies and we begin to feel more in control of ourselves.

The very best exercise when you are in pain or upset or anxious or feeling out of control is also the simplest. Breathe. Stop whatever you are doing and take three very deep breaths. As you inhale deeply, think of strength, energy, and the life force going into you. This is what is really happening; now focus on it. Hold your breath and then slowly exhale. As you exhale, imagine that all the stress, tension, and anxiety are being released from your body. After three deep breaths you will feel calmer and more in control. Your body will be more relaxed. You will be able to function better.

Another simple exercise is walking. Take a brisk walk around the block or around a track or gym. Walking helps thinking. If your mind is scattered and you feel really anxious, focus on what you are seeing as you are walking. Give yourself a break and take a time-out. Some things cannot be solved immediately. Stop feeling that you are under pressure and must change what you are feeling. Allow yourself a little time and do something active. It will help.

Self-Esteem means loving yourself *and* taking care of yourself. When you are in a bad place, do whatever you can to get to a better place. Exercising is one tool to help you make the transition. Think about yourself when you are experiencing joy—how difficult it is to sit still and how much natural movement your body makes.

Passive exercise, such as meditation, also helps. Anything which will temporarily take you out of yourself and allow you to observe objectively what is happening to you is an antidote to the anxiety and the pain of the moment. These things are not an escape and not a denial, unless overused, but they do tend to lessen the helplessness and hopelessness of the moment. Use them. They are tools that work.

III. Individual Issues

I've been doing this all my life; why change now?

Because it no longer works. We do not change when life is working for us. We only change when something is going wrong. The problem with the Doing Model is that it works—for a while. When it stops working, we tend to believe that something is wrong with us and not with the model. Usually, when we are feeling good about our lives and about ourselves, we are not seeking change. When we are looking for new answers, something is not working.

Timing is everything and we all have our own time. We will feel the need to change only when it is our time to change. We will know when this time occurs because we will be in pain and we will be willing to try something new and different to alleviate the pain. If we are not in pain but are merely curious about learning the new Model of Being, most likely we will not change anything. Curiosity is not a good incentive for change. Pain is.

If this is not your time for change, accept that and love yourself for being where you are. If this is your time, know that the change will also be painful but that the pain of change is cleansing and leads to growth. Growth is development and development means letting go of things that have worked before but now do not. Development means learning new things that are strange and sometimes frightening. Let go of the idea that there is something wrong with you because you can no longer function in the same ways that you always have before.

No one else can decide when it is your time to change. You will change and the new tools will make sense when, and only when, it is your time. You may be experiencing feeling stuck; you want to change, you feel that you are ready to change, but nothing is happening. During these times, it is easy to get frustrated and go back to your previous training. You may become goal oriented and feel you are a failure because you cannot achieve your goal to change. Change is inevitable but it is not in your total control. Neither is your timing. When you are stuck and do not understand why, the best thing to do is to accept yourself as stuck and practice loving yourself in your stuck place. This is not easy but it works. Eventually you will not remain stuck. You will move and change will occur.

Also, do not get caught in the blame of why it has taken you so long to change. Blaming yourself for something you cannot control will throw you right back into Weak Ego. Remember, this is not a contest and you have no competitors. It does not matter how quickly you change or how well you love yourself. The Being Model is not quantitative. Where you are is where you are. You will always change. You cannot control the timing. You can control the ways in which you change. Do not waste your time feeling bad about why you have not changed before or why you are stuck now. Accept your timing just as you have learned to accept yourself. If everything is working for you, good. If nothing is working for you, that is also good. You are probably closer to your time for changing.

Why am I so angry?

Anger is one of the most basic and also most important emotions. It is necessary for survival as the feeling often generates the necessary strength to do things to protect ourselves that we normally could not do. Anger is also necessary in the infant's development of a sense of self as distinct from others. Everyone has anger. Why then is this important emotion so difficult for people to deal with? Why does anger produce so much denial of the feeling? And so much fear?

The answers, once again, go back to our training. We have been taught, since we were little, that being angry is "bad" and that other people do not like us when we are angry. We learned that most of our anger is unjustified (as if feelings need justification) and that we have no right to be angry because we must consider the other person's feelings before we consider ourselves. We have learned as children to deny our feelings of anger and to repress them so that we will not be labeled "bad." If we cannot deny or repress the anger and we let it out, then we feel guilty and have to make justifications for our feelings. We have learned, usually before the age of five, that anger produces a vicious trap: if we express it, we are "bad," if we repress it, it grows into rage and we are "bad," and if we deny it, we learn not to trust our own feelings and that feels "bad." What is the solution to this anger trap?

Give yourself permission to feel angry. You cannot control your feelings of anger. You do not always know when and why and how you will feel angry. Sometimes you may feel angry without knowing why. And sometimes, when you would expect to feel angry, you do not. Anger lives inside of you along with your other feelings. Accept that you can feel angry. But do not confuse the feeling of anger with the expression of anger. You cannot control the feeling of anger but you can control what you choose to do when you are angry.

Our training has taught us to confuse the feeling of anger with the angry behaviors that we exhibit. Most of us are afraid of what we do when we are angry. We have repressed and denied our anger until it explodes and we are in a rage. We then act in a destructive manner, to others and to ourselves. Accepting the angry feeling as it occurs means that we do not accumulate the feelings until they become rage. Often, accepting our anger as it occurs is enough. Remember, we do not always have to act on our feelings and our thoughts. We can choose what we will do and we have a wide variety of choices.

Practice saying to yourself when you feel angry: "I am angry. What do I want to do with this? How can I feel okay with my anger?" Sometimes you may choose to express it to others. Sometimes you may choose to think about it for a while before you act on it. Sometimes you may want to yell and get upset and sometimes you may want to calmly talk it out. And, once in a while, you may choose to let it go and to do nothing about it. There is no one right way to act when angry. Any behavior you choose is right as long as you take responsibility for it and you feel all right with yourself. If you cannot get past your anger and let it go, ask for help. Most of the time, recognizing that you are angry at the moment you feel it and accepting your feeling without judgment is enough for the feeling to abate. Just as you cannot control your feelings, your feelings cannot control you, unless you choose to let them.

Why do I feel that I am out of control?

We feel out of control when we do not trust ourselves. We also feel out of control when we let our feelings overwhelm us and we do not take responsibility for our actions. Feeling out of control and feeling insecure both come from the same source—a lack of Self-Esteem. We feel unable to do the best we can and we often externalize the reasons for our lack of self-control. Someone or something else is responsible for the way we are. We have given our personal power away. We have become reactors to external sources.

Next time you feel out of control, think of an elevator. An elevator reacts when someone pushes the button. Anyone can come along and push the up button and you feel angry or the down button and you feel depressed. The only way to stop working as an elevator is to put up an "out of order" sign. Stop reacting to what others want you to do.

Do not be someone else's victim. No one else has the right to your personal power. Just as you cannot control anyone else, no one else can control you unless you give them that illusion. You cannot be a good elevator because you cannot take other people where they want to go. You can only take yourself where you need to be and you cannot do this if you feel out of control.

Stop the blame-game. Do not blame others or yourself. Be responsible for feeling out of control. It is your choice and now you know that you have other choices. Try something different. Act rather than react. Get out of the victim role and do not allow anyone or anything else to push your buttons. If you know in advance how others are going to act and how they will try to push your buttons, be prepared by imagining that your buttons are out of order. Do something different. Act first before they act. Use your objective eyes to perceive what they are doing and do not internalize their behaviors. What others do is their choice. Ask yourself why they are making that choice. Is it possible that they are as insecure as you and need you to react in order to justify themselves? People who need victims, who need to push buttons in others, are not people who have Self-Esteem. Self-Esteemed ones will not take your power even if you try to give it to them. They will not reinforce your reacting behaviors but will encourage your taking control of yourself. They will never want you in the victim role. They do not need you to be their elevator.

Choose to exert control over what you can control—your feelings about yourself and your behaviors. Get out of the elevator business!

Why am I depressed?

One way to define depression is that our anger has turned inward, against ourselves, until everything becomes self-defeating. Depression exists when our thoughts, our perceptions, and our observations of reality begin to match the negative expectations that we have created for ourselves and for our world. People become depressed when they are not en-couraged, reinforced, and taught to believe that they are good. Sensitive people often respond to all the negativity in this crazy world by internalizing it and becoming depressed.

It is important to note that there are many types of depression but the two main sources are genetic/physiological and situational/ adjustment reactions. Those of us who have a family history of depression and who are frequently depressed without reason may need to be evaluated for physiological causes. In these cases, medication can often provide relief from what is genetically at fault. Trying to talk ourselves out of our depressions with only therapy, or using role models and support from others, is similar to trying to talk ourselves out of a vitamin deficiency. In these cases, our development of Self-Esteem will be severely hampered by a biological impediment. Antidepressants work, and when we do have physiological depressions, using these medications, along with support and therapy, makes the most sense. Genetic depression is not a personal weakness and it is not something that we can conquer by willpower. It is similar to the color of our eyes in that we were born with this trait and it is out of our control. Seeking help from all available resources, including medication, puts the depression within our control.

The other main source of depression is situational. This means that we are being affected by something in our environment. There are many good reasons to be sad and it is a human response to be depressed when we encounter loss and trauma and pain. But this type of depression, caused by loss, is similar to pain in that it will decrease over time. Chronic depression is different; this does not pass over time but takes over our lives and becomes the only way we perceive the world—through depressive eyes.

Chronically depressed people are angry and self-centered. They do not have any sense of their own personal power and they do not feel strong enough to take responsibility for themselves. The people around them know how much negative power these depressives exert. These people are very difficult to love because they turn away from love either for themselves or for others. Chronic depression is not a feeling like sadness. It may be an absence of all feelings or an overwhelming combination of all feelings together which produces a lack of feeling. Chronic depression may feel hopeless but it is not. People can and do get over their depressions.

If you are chronically depressed, accept it and stop the blame. It helps enormously to want to be over the depression. Realize that you are not only feeling depressed but that you are also behaving in a depressed manner. You can change your behaviors and your feelings will follow. Drag yourself out of your depression long enough to seek help. Try courage—do something different even though you do not want to or do not have the energy to do it. Do it anyway and reward yourself for being courageous. Recognize that your perceptions of yourself and the world are just that, perceptions, and are not the reality. You can change the way you perceive things. Try to learn observing eyes. Become self-ish and take yourself out of the center. It takes time but you have time.

Why am I so afraid of my feelings?

As mentioned before, we have been taught to confuse our feelings with the expressions of our feelings. We think that our feelings are synonymous with the behaviors we exhibit. Therefore, anger becomes yelling, fear becomes shaking, and sadness becomes crying. However, feelings are one thing and behaviors are another. We can be angry without yelling, afraid without shaking, and sad without crying.

We also have been taught to confuse what we can control. We have been trained to try to control our anger, fear, joy, and so on. We have been told that it is not appropriate to be angry in certain situations and that we cannot be sad without being weak. How often have we heard parents tell their children, "Don't be sad." "You can't be angry at me." "Don't get so excited," and so forth. And so we grow up thinking that we must somehow control what we feel but not knowing how to do this. It becomes easier to try not to feel than to feel at inappropriate times. And when we cannot control our feelings, we become guilty and punish ourselves for being out of control. It is no wonder that we think of our feelings as enemies and become afraid of them!

Since you cannot control your feelings, it is an exercise in futility to try. Focus instead on accepting your feelings without fear and practice controlling your expressions of these feelings. This may be easier than it sounds. There is time between the awareness of what you are feeling and your behavior. Begin noticing this time period. When you behave instantly in response to your feelings, you are reacting and will often feel that your feelings have taken control over you. Realize that there is no need for an instant reaction. Take the time to choose how you want to express yourself. Acknowledge your feeling by stating, "I am feeling _____"; angry or sad or whatever. Then ask yourself, "What do I need to do?" Then take a few seconds more and ask yourself, "How will I feel about myself after I do this?" If you think that you will feel bad, do not do it. Try something else. If you think you will feel all right, then do it. If you are not sure, try not doing anything. It is okay to be unsure. If someone else is involved, tell the other person what you are feeling and that you do not know what to do. Often they will help solve your confusion by the way they respond to you. You may begin a dialogue in a way that requires no other action. Remember that recognizing your feeling and accepting it means that you will no longer be afraid of the feeling. All your feelings, the ones you like and the ones you do not like, are normal and natural. They are part of you and they are not good or bad, right or wrong. Feelings are what separate humans from machines. Do not be afraid of your humanness and you will no longer fear your emotions.

I have everything I need; why am I miserable?

This answer requires the definition of "everything." When this question is asked, "everything" inevitably means all the externals that society, the western model, defines as important. And all these externals are related to the Weak Ego, the things outside of ourselves which give us esteem. All these external things are not connected to the internal self, the part of us that has Self-Esteem, because of their transient and temporary nature. Everything is not anything when it is outside of our control and can leave us at any moment.

External things do not satisfy the inner self or the inner child. They are toys which soon lose their value. Often we discover that the real fun occurs when we are trying to achieve them and that once we own these externals, they lose their value to us and we go off in search of something else to acquire. The fun is in the challenge and not the acquisition of the thing itself. This is just the opposite case in the search for Self-Esteem. The challenge is there but the real joy comes with the acquisition. And the longer we have Self-Esteem, the more we value it.

All the external things, the Weak Ego things, are not the meaningful things for the internal self or to the inner child. Neither our
self nor our inner child wants to have goodies in place of love. The
paradox here is that the more goodies we throw at our internal self
and our inner child, the more the internal self gets lost and the
inner child starves. The Doing Model values these goodies and
teaches us that we should feel satisfaction when we are successful.
Success is defined by things and the more successful you are, the
more things you have. These external things become addictive until
we are no longer satisfied with anything we have and everything
becomes unimportant. Think of some rich people that we may
know, rich in the sense of the western model. How many of them
enjoy what they have? How many of them can say "enough . . . I
have enough"? How many houses, how many cars, how many
clothes does it take to feel good about ourselves? How much
money does it take to love ourselves? The western model refuses to
answer these questions. As a matter of fact, once we ask these
questions, we are off the model. The answers, of course, are not in
this model.

The answers to all the questions are simple: You cannot buy Self-
Esteem. You cannot acquire it from externals. And you cannot be
content without it. Having everything you need, when everything
is defined as outside of you, usually leads to being cynical, critical,
and jaded. Nothing seems sadder than the very rich Weak Ego.
These poor souls really believe in the western model and they
really do not understand why they feel miserable. Often they try to
do more, to set higher goals, to have unrealistic expectations for
themselves and others. They work faster and feel too important.
And when they finally see the reality of themselves and their lives,
often it is overwhelming.

It is ridiculous to search for something in a place where you did
not lose it. Stop looking for Self-Esteem in the Weak Ego model. If
you have "everything" and you are miserable, why not try some-

thing new? You can enjoy what toys you have to play with as long as you do not have unrealistic expectations of what your toys will do for you. Play with your toys when you want to but take the time to work on yourself by developing Self-Esteem. Do not expect your toys to give you inner awareness and balance and self-worth. Remember, they are only toys. They are not you. And you, and only you, are responsible for how you feel about yourself.

Why am I so resentful?

Resentment occurs when we are not giving enough to ourselves. It means that we are giving too much of ourselves away to others and that we are feeling empty, lonely, abused, misused, whatever. Resentment is not defined as a true feeling. It is a feeling, probably anger or sadness, that has been rationalized or intellectualized by our "computer brain" into what we call resentment. In order to deal with resentment, it is easier to get to the source of it—to get to the underlying feelings.

Resentment occurs when we give an "unclean" gift, a gift that has strings attached. For example, we give something, our time, our energy, or maybe a tangible thing, that we do not really want to give or that we are giving for a reason. We are giving something in order to get something back and the purpose of the giving is the getting back. We expect our gift to have rewards. We wait for our expected reward and when it does not occur, we feel resentful. We are angry that we have given our gift and we are angry at the receiver of the gift. They have not followed through and lived up to our expectations and we are resentful. We would like to take our gift back.

Resentment can only occur when you are not taking care of

yourself. Remember the cookie jar theory: if you only bake cookies for others and never bake cookies for yourself, you will feel resentment when others eat your cookies. You will not feel resentful if you are filling your own needs. Before you give a gift to someone else, give a gift to yourself. Take care of your own needs first and then your gifts will be clean.

Resentment is probably the second most self-destructive concept, after guilt. Resentment can be thought of as the cancer of the spirit. It is almost impossible to love or want to be around a resentful person. It is the opposite of responsible. Resentment means waiting for someone else to know what we need, to act on our needs, and to take care of us. And when others do not do these things, when others cannot do these things for us, resentment occurs to externalize the blame.

Think of resentment as the disease of the addict. Everything we are and everything we need has been externalized. We are no longer responsible for the way we feel. Someone else is. We have become martyrs in that we give and give to others but no one is giving back to us. The addict is waiting for something external to fix him or her. The addict feels justified in being angry at a delayed fix. The addict feels justified in blaming the external world for his or her problems. The addict is truly self-centered. When we feel resentment, we act like addicts. We are refusing to take responsibility for our behaviors. The gifts we give to others are too costly. They are manipulative and demand a much higher gift back.

If you are resentful, begin to change by focusing on what you need, rather than what you are giving. Take care of your own needs. Try to stop being angry because others do not know what you need or do not give it to you. Stop taking care of others. Stop being codependent. Seek help. Think of your resentment as a cancer. Many cancers can now be cured. Your resentment can be cured. Who would choose to have cancer when they can be cancer free? Be prepared to do whatever it takes to get rid of your resentful feelings. You will have to try new behaviors and you will have to take care of yourself. You would do this if you had cancer; do it to get rid of resentment. It eats away at your soul and stops you from having Self-Esteem. Who needs it?

Why am I so confused about everything?

Hurray! Being in the state of confusion occurs when we are in the right place and time to learn something new. Being confused about everything means that the western model no longer works for us. The model no longer answers what we need. It means that reacting to others no longer works and that something fundamental is missing from our lives. Being confused means that what we have been taught no longer answers our instinctive questions. Being confused means that we are ripe to accept a new concept. Confusion is a normal state of being human and being imperfect. The state of confusion is a necessary antecedent for change. We do not change when we are sure of where we are. We only change when we are uncomfortable, in pain, and confused.

Welcome confusion. Know that it is the beginning of something new. Confusion means uncertainty. It means that we are willing to take a risk and try something unfamiliar. But most of all, it means that we are ready for change. The western model teaches us that it is important to always be in control, even of things we cannot control. Confusion means that we are no longer comfortable with the model. It sets the stage for risk taking. If we were not confused, then we would not be willing to change.

Think of how confusing it must be to be an infant in a world that she or he does not understand and that she or he has not yet learned to communicate with. What does the infant do? She or he tries everything, and everything is a new behavior, to make sense of the environment and he or she risks all to communicate. And it works. The infant learns how to communicate, how to get along, and how to do what he or she needs to do. No matter how old we are chronologically, we are all infants when we begin to learn how to have Self-Esteem.

If you are confused, take all risks. Try anything that will work. And if one thing does not work, try another. Eventually you will come to the conclusion that you cannot find what you need outside of yourself. You will discover that all paths lead to the same place and that place is the center of yourself. If you want to learn how not to be confused, study the concept of paradox. Accept yourself as confused and allow yourself to be uncertain. As soon as you do this, you will be less confused. Rejoice in your confusion as a positive vehicle for change and as soon as you rejoice, you will become less confused. Look for the answers within yourself, and you will become more secure that the answers are there. Enjoy your confusion and let go of the idea that you have any control over it. As soon as you let go, you will become more sure of yourself. Paradox works. Confusion is a positive state. It means that you are human and that you do not know all the answers and that you are okay. You cannot be confused and also believe that you are perfect. You cannot be confused and be the victim of the Weak Ego. The state of confusion is similar to the state of grace; when you give in and accept that you do not know and are not all powerful, you are closer to God than when you are not confused and think you know.

I sometimes have crazy thoughts; does this mean I am crazy?

We are all crazy to some degree. Being human means being somewhat crazy. Creativity is a more acceptable word for craziness. Creative means being outside of the norm, outside of the box, outside of the western model. We all know that true genius means seeing the world in a different way, in a crazy way. Psychology, psychiatry, the medical establishment define craziness by function and behavior, not by thought alone. We can have crazy thoughts but if we do not act on them and if we do not allow them to control our lives, we will probably not be labeled as crazy. The best example of this is the story of an inmate confined to a mental hospital. His psychologist told him to preface everything he thought with the statement, "I dreamed that _____" and soon he was released from the hospital. It is perfectly acceptable to have crazy dreams as long as we do not believe that they are real. So it is with our thoughts. We are responsible for our behaviors and these we can control.

No one knows exactly where the boundaries for crazy begin. We do know that the norm sets the mid-range and that if you think and behave as most others think and behave, you will not be labeled crazy. Therefore, true brilliance is often labeled craziness because it is outside the limits set by the norm.

This is not to say that pathology, real craziness, does not exist. It most certainly does. This type of pathology is defined as those who cannot function in an adaptive or acceptable manner. Pathology also clearly exists when there is no conscience, no awareness of others. We have discussed the dangers of being too aware of others to the point of excluding the self. But there is a balance between being too aware of others and not at all aware of others. Both ends of this continuum result in being labeled a form of crazy: being too aware of others is a sickness called codependent. Being not at all aware means being either psychotic or narcissistic. The difference between being psychotic or being neurotic (having a personality disorder) depends on the degree to which we function in the world. If we can function well in some capacities (i.e., work) but not in others (i.e., relationships), we are labeled as having a personality disorder. If we cannot function well in any capacity due to a pervasive illness such as paranoia or schizophrenia, we are labeled psychotic. If we do not have the horsepower to function at all, we are labeled mentally deficient. If we function brilliantly but differently, we are called eccentric or genius. There are labels for everything outside the norm. Even "normal" is a label.

At some time or other, you will have crazy thoughts. Recognize that your thoughts are like your feelings, not in your control. But what you do with these thoughts, whether you choose to act on them or not, is in your control. Do not be afraid of your crazy thoughts. Some of them may be brilliant. Others may be just crazy. Some may be induced by fever or alternate states of consciousness. You do not have to act on any of your thoughts. If you choose to act on your thoughts, you are then responsible for your behavior. Thinking something does not mean it will happen or that you have to make it happen. You do not have to attend to all of your thoughts. You do have to be aware of how you behave. It is acceptable to have crazy thoughts as long as they remain just that, crazy thoughts. It is not acceptable to have crazy behaviors. You are responsible for what you choose to do and how you behave. Self-Esteem means acting in a loving way to yourself and to others.

Why am I so critical (judgmental)?

Criticism of others reflects our own level of insecurity. It is impossible to accept others, and their weaknesses and mistakes, if we cannot accept ourselves. The more unsure we are about ourselves, the more we look for faults in others. This is one way of excusing our own faults; we justify ourselves by criticizing others. It is as if we are saying: "I'm not so bad, just look at him, he's worse."

The western model seems to need comparison with others and judgment of everything and everyone as part of the competitive edge that we have been taught to acquire as a means to success. We have learned to measure our success by comparing what we have relative to what others have or do. Often, we criticize others to help us feel more secure about ourselves. It is easier to judge others as imperfect and focus on their weaknesses than it is to take a hard look at our own behaviors. Besides, everyone else is doing this and criticism of others seems to be an ordinary, and often interesting, part of human communication. "Let me tell you what he did," insures an interested audience. And isn't all gossip dependent to some degree on criticism or judgment?

One problem with judging others is that while it may tend to make us feel better to focus on others' faults rather than our own and it may seem to lessen our own insecurities, it is a very short-lived remedy. All too soon we become aware that if we are saying all this negative stuff about someone, what are others saying about us? As soon as we recognize that we are not immune from being judged and criticized, our insecurities increase, our defenses go up and we become even more critical and judgmental. And the negative circle becomes more vicious and we become more insecure and the Weak Ego is in full control.

Judging other people, saying bad things about them, putting people down, gossiping, comparing, and being negative all contribute to the state of discouragement. No one wants to remain for a long time around discouraging people. Also, putting ourselves down, comparing and finding ourselves to be less than everyone else, putting others on pedestals so that we look bad—all are aspects of judging but this time we are on the lower end of the criticisms and we are vocalizing our own lack of security. We become discouraging to ourselves. And discouragement, either of others or of self, is one of the most destructive behaviors to the human spirit. We cannot begin to do our best when we are in a discouraged state.

Judgment and criticism are closely related to expectations. Generally, we criticize when we expect something to occur and it does not. It is typical to want people to do things for us or to take care of us or to be as we perceive them, and when they fall short or do not measure up to our expectations then we feel the criticism is warranted. After all, they did not do what they were "supposed" to do. Think about this process for a moment. Whose eyes are doing the judging? Who is setting the standards? Who is assuming that they have the right perceptions? Judging others implies comparing them to something and who has the right to know what that ultimate something is? When we criticize or judge others, are we not perceiving the world through self-centered eyes? Are we not implicitly imposing our standards or beliefs or failures on others?

All judgment and criticism, of ourselves or of others, implies the need for perfection. Once we give this up, once we accept that no one can be perfect, then we no longer need to engage in the destructive and discouraging practice of judging others. We can accept and let others be. We can become encouragers.

Why am I so possessive?

Being possessive of things or of people is another way of demonstrating our own insecurities. It means that we are trying to fulfill our own needs from external sources. We become possessive when we are unsure of ourselves and need others or things to convince us of our self-worth. The western model has taught us that our worth is determined by what we possess and we have learned to focus on external rather than internal possessions. We become possessive of someone else's love when we do not know how to love ourselves. We become collectors of things when we do not feel convinced that we are enough.

Everything outside of ourselves is not ours. It may be on loan to us for a period of time but it is not ours to keep. When we are possessive, we often try to keep these things, to cling to them. The paradox here is that clinging to something frequently results in losing it. If we have ever been loved by a possessive person, then we know how destructive their clinging becomes. Possessiveness fosters jealousy and jealousy destroys what it purports to love. It is very difficult to act in a loving way and to encourage growth when we are afraid of losing the object of that so-called love.

Possessive love is not real love; rather, it describes real need. And needing someone results in far different behaviors than really loving them. When we are possessive, we are trying to resist change. We are trying to keep things as they are, and in so doing we are creating an artificial reality of life. We are focusing our time and energy on being loved rather than on giving love. Possessiveness is an emotional handicap because it means using an external crutch to find self-worth. What we are possessive of owns us. It becomes a burden and stops us from loving ourselves. We not only destroy the object of our possessiveness, but we also destroy ourselves in the process.

The only way to stop being possessive, of others and of things, is to take care of your own needs to be loved and esteemed. Try to give to yourself what you need from the other person. Imagine yourself without anything and focus on what you have inside of you. This may sound terrifying if all your worth has been focused externally, but you do have everything you need inside of yourself. Stop perceiving the world through self-centered eyes. You are not the center of anything except yourself. No matter how much you have externally, you have nothing if you cannot love yourself. Become possessive of your own time and energy. Become self-ish. Try to do for yourself what you rely on others to do for you. The next time you feel possessive of someone, the next time you want someone to reassure you, try doing it for yourself.

Let the people and the things you love be. Do not expect them to fill your needs. There is a wonderful paradox here: the less possessive you are, the more loved you will be. The less you need others, the more they will want to be around you. Secure people, those with Self-Esteem, do not have the time or energy to be possessive. They are too busy and too content to put their needs on anyone else and they accept the fact that others do not want to take care of them. Remember, you cannot be possessive and also have Self-Esteem. Possessiveness is about needs; Self-Esteem is about love and choices. Possessiveness is a prison; Self-Esteem is freedom. Which do you choose?

Why am I always crying? (Or, why do I never cry?)

These two questions may seem to be the opposite of each other but like many opposites, they result from the same cause. Too much crying or the inability to cry at all mean that there is a lack of trust in ourselves and that we are trying to control our feelings. We have been trained not to trust ourselves, our feelings, and we have also been taught that we have to control these feelings. We grow up believing that giving in to our feelings is wrong and that we are weak if we do so. We cry too much when we do not trust that we can take care of ourselves. We never cry at all when we are afraid of our tears. Both reflect the fear that we cannot control ourselves.

When we are crying all the time, we have probably lost sight of why we are crying at all. We have given up and given in and feel hopeless and lost. We become afraid that we are stuck in the sadness of life. When we never cry at all, we are also afraid—afraid of being out of control and being helpless. The price for our overcontrol is not to feel and not to feel is not to be fully alive. Both crying all the time and never crying at all are not real. Tears when we are sad or moved or very happy are as natural as blowing our noses when we have a cold. By natural processes, our colds will pass. So will our tears if we allow the natural process to work.

The person who is stoic and the person who cries all the time are both stuck. They no longer believe in the natural process. They both are overusing and overgeneralizing one response, one defense, one way of being to all situations. They are working very hard to avoid the reality of living. In the short term, both reactions may work. Other people may rush in to take care of the crier and they may praise the stoic for his control. After a short while, however, both of these responses become tiresome. The crier may be told to pull himself together and the stoic may find that no one can relate to him. What to do?

Stop hating the tears—either the abundance or the lack of them. Give yourself permission to cry or permission not to cry. Accept that you have been trained by a faulty model but do not blame the model. Try not to blame yourself. By giving yourself permission to do something you are already doing, you begin the process of acceptance. And an interesting phenomenon usually occurs—the opposite begins to happen. If you give yourself permission to cry when you are crying, you begin to feel more in control of yourself. You are allowing yourself to cry and you no longer feel guilty about your behavior. The same holds true when you give yourself permission not to cry. After you have given yourself permission to do what you are already doing, give yourself permission to do the opposite. Tell yourself, "I will stop crying when I need to stop" or "I will cry when I need to cry." This may sound crazy and much too simplistic but it often works.

You may become stuck with a behavior when you hate yourself for that behavior. You may also get stuck when you are afraid of the behavior. Separate the feeling from the behavior. Let the feeling be and focus on the behavior. Crying is a behavior. Tears are a natural response to your feeling and as part of a natural process, they will abate. Crying too much or not crying at all mean that you have interfered with the natural process. Trust yourself and trust the process. Acknowledge the feeling that is generating the tears. Allow yourself to feel and to respond with tears. Take care of yourself and trust that your tears will stop. Tears do not mean weakness; they mean that you are human.

Why can't I stand up for myself?

The fear of being assertive, or "standing up" for ourselves, is most often related to our training on how to be "good" or "nice." Because our training has not taught us how to love ourselves, we have focused our time and energies on people-pleasing behaviors in order to be loved. We have been trained to believe that others will become angry and withdraw from us if we express opinions contrary to what they are saying. It becomes easier to agree and withhold our own rights, choices, and feelings rather than risk abandonment. We think that if we "go along" then we will be loved and taken care of by these others. The paradox here is that usually people-pleasers become a pain to those around them. People stop believing in all that niceness and begin to wonder if there is a real person in there. And people who never assert themselves become a lot of work for others because no one, including the people-pleaser, knows what they really want or need or feel. The end result is usually exactly what the people-pleaser is trying to avoid —abandonment, either emotionally or physically.

Not standing up for ourselves means exactly that—literally and figuratively. It means that we do not feel worthy to be in this world and to hold opinions and thoughts and feelings and rights. Asserting ourselves means putting ourselves forward and expressing who we are. It does not mean being pushy or aggressive. The bully is as insecure as the people-pleaser and it is no coincidence how these opposites attract each other. We can easily recognize how the bully is self-centered but can we also recognize the self-centeredness in the people-pleaser? This person has delegated their rights to take care of themselves to others. They have bartered their ability to love themselves by expecting others to love them because of their nice behaviors. They try to have others around them assume the responsibility for their lives by never taking charge of their own lives. They are self-centered because they are using their people-pleasing behaviors to fulfill their own needs. These people are more concerned with *appearing* nice than they are with dealing with the reality of life. They begin by being lovingly manipulative, doing something in order to get something back, and end by being resentful and feeling abused.

Niceness is not the same as goodness. Being passive, going along when you don't want to, agreeing when you secretly disagree have a high price. These people-pleasing behaviors do not work. They stop us from being real and from doing the best we can. They stop others from trusting us and from relating with us in an honest way. Not being assertive leads to resentment—resentment within ourselves for not having our needs met and resentment in others for having to take care of us. It is not real to always be nice. It creates a complicated and eventually destructive circle of negative behaviors.

Stop being so damned nice. Say what you really think and feel. The world will not fall apart when you really express yourself. The paradox is that being real and open and honest are much more simple than being what you think other people want you to be. Remember that others have the right to choose and they may not choose to agree with you. Allow yourself to disagree, to stand up for yourself, and allow others to do the same. This results in a much simpler and saner way of being. No matter how nice you try to be, everyone will not love you. That is okay if you love yourself. And the people who do love you will know and love the real you and that is the only one worth knowing. Assert yourself. Stand up for yourself. You are here and you are real. Let the world know it.

Why can't I say "No"?

For obvious reasons, this question is related to the previous question about standing up for ourselves. People who cannot say "No" often do not know what they want or do not want. Frequently, these people think that "No" is a dirty word and that others will not like them if they say it. Being able to say "No" clearly and to mean it are indicators of respecting the self. Doing this means that we are able to take care of our own needs. Not being able to say "No" frequently means that we do not know what we do not want and we also do not know what we do want. It is not a coincidence that "yes people" end up feeling angry, confused, and used, and not knowing exactly how they got that way.

It is also not a coincidence that people who never say "No" end up with people who rarely say "Yes" to them. These kinds of opposites really do attract each other and together they create a dysfunctional unit. Not being able to say "No" means that we do not trust ourselves—we do not trust that we have rights and needs. It means that we have become more concerned with what other people want and need than we have with ourselves.

People who cannot say "No" are dancing in other people's

heads. This means that they are trying to figure out how to take care of others and, in order to do so, they have to try to figure out what motivates the other person. They are trying to passively coerce the other person into taking care of them. This sounds like manipulation and it is. By never saying "No" to anyone else's demands or needs, we are expecting them to never say "No" to our own demands and needs. Furthermore, we are expecting them to dance in our heads and to know what we want and need even when we do not. The fact of the matter is that no one can really be in someone else's head; there is only room for one person per head and that is the person who owns the head. Dancing in someone else's head means that we are not spending time in our own heads. It means that we are not taking care of ourselves. It also means that we cannot know what we need and want.

Dance in your own head. Say "No" when you think that you do not want to do what is asked of you. Only say "Yes" to someone else when you are sure that you are giving a clean gift, a gift without strings. This means that you really want to do what is asked or expected of you and that you expect *nothing* back in return. Does this sound self-ish? Good, it is. Does this sound self-centered? Only if you do not ever want to do anything for anyone else but you expect them to do everything for you.

People who cannot say "No" are generally very nice people who are trying to be good. These people tend to confuse being nice with being good. They really want to be genuinely helpful and they do not understand why their system produces so much anger and resentment. Once again, the solution lies in faulty training. There is another paradox here and that is that people who can never say "No" are not usually respected by others. Their nice behaviors are taken for granted and they are treated as victims or as not very important. People respect a "No" answer and when they then get a "Yes" answer at another time, they appreciate it more and know that it is real.

Practice saying "No." The world will not fall apart when you do so. Be clear in expressing how you feel. It makes life much simpler for you and for others. You will be surprised at how much people respect a clean, clear *"No"* and you will feel better about yourself for being truthful and for taking care of yourself. Everyone will win!

How can I stop abusing alcohol? Drugs? Food? Sex? Others? Myself?

Abuse is always an addictive behavior. We abuse things in order to stop the pain of life and to make us momentarily feel better—stronger, more in control—or to escape from the reality of our lives. Because abusive behavior gives us a sense of control or fosters the illusion of escape for the moment, we repeat the behavior. But abuse always generates guilt and guilt produces a vicious circle. It is like a snake with its tail in its mouth, which was discussed in the earlier question about guilt. We do something that we know is wrong or bad, then we feel guilty about it and this feeling of guilt is a panacea. At first, we are relieved that we are feeling guilty because that means that we are really not bad people because we have learned that "bad people" do not feel guilt. But after a while the guilt keeps growing and the pain of the guilt becomes intolerable. Then we begin to externalize and justify our guilt. We say things like: "I wouldn't have done that if he had not done what he did" or "She made me do that" or "They just don't understand me." All too soon our rationalizations or defenses begin to sound so reasonable and our behavior so justified, that we do it again.

This is the vicious circle of addiction, guilt, justification, and more addiction. This is the circular snake.

All addictions, all abuse of self or others, have one thing in common. They are all a product of insecurity about yourself. They are all a way to try to externalize your lack of love for yourself. You cannot love yourself and behave in loving ways to yourself and also abuse yourself. You also cannot really love others and abuse them and yourself around them. All abuse, all addictions, are first and foremost, self-centered. They mean that you are perceiving the world only through the eyes of your own needs. They mean that your insecurities, your Weak Ego, are so powerful that they totally control your behaviors.

The most successful interventions for abusive and addictive behaviors are those that replace the destructive behavior with a constructive one. In other words, you replace a "bad" addiction with a "good" addiction. Alcoholics replace the alcohol with AA, drug addicts replace the drug with a twelve-step program. So it is with food, sex, and other forms of abuse. The abusive behaviors are replaced with a constructive behavior. Twelve-step programs work because they fill the void when you decide to give up the addiction. They give you something else to focus upon and they give you a place to spend your time and energy.

There is something else that the supportive group gives you that may even be more important than replacing the addiction. The group gives you an en-couraging environment which is essential to avoid the dis-couragement that the addiction feeds upon. These twelve-step programs become role models for how to stop the self-abuse. They accept you as you are, a human in pain, and they do not expect you to be perfect. Rather, they emphasize that you cannot be perfect and that you can turn yourself and your addiction over to a Higher Power. You do not have to be strong in order to conquer your addiction. You do not have to become perfect. Twelve-step programs are an excellent way to learn Self-Esteem.

Twelve-step groups, like all good support groups, are very power-ful therapy. They are more powerful than the addiction and the self-abuse if you let them be. By accepting you as you are, the group teaches you to accept yourself. By encouraging you to be the best you can be, the support group becomes a positive role model for self-love.

I was an abused child—why do I abuse myself?

Most of us have been abused emotionally; too many of us have been abused physically or sexually. We may think that because we have been abused by others, we would go out of our way not to abuse ourselves. In actuality, just the opposite occurs. Abused children tend to grow up into abusive adults. This is a good example of how powerful our training has been. We have been taught not to value ourselves and not to take care of our own needs. We are good students of our early training and we tend to follow the script that has been written for us. This script dictates that we are not worthy of being treated well, that we are "bad" and need to be punished. Our early abuse robs us of our basic integrity and awareness of our innate goodness. It teaches us that we have a terrible dark side that we must be afraid of. Abuse teaches us not to trust ourselves, that we don't deserve to be safe and secure and loved. It kills our spirit and stops our risk-taking tendencies. We learn to repress our own feelings and to manipulate others to get our needs met. Abuse is a terrible teacher. The abusive script is a lose-lose situation that produces a vicious and dangerous cycle.

The teacher can be overruled and the script can be discarded. This does not have to be a hopeless situation.

The way out of this abusive cycle is to begin with the realization that you did not write this script and you do not have to live it. You are not responsible for your early training and it is not your fault that you were abused. You did not deserve it. You could not control it. You are completely blameless. No matter how difficult a child you may have been, you did not merit being abused. No one does. There can be no question about who was wrong—the person who abused you was wrong. Completely. You must accept that you were a victim and that you have nothing to be ashamed of or to hide. You do not have to forgive yourself for something that was not your fault. Let go of all guilt—it is not yours. Repeat to yourself many times: "It was not my fault!" until you really believe this. This is a critical first step.

The second step out of the script is to recognize that you are good. No matter what you have done or what has been done to you, you are good. This goodness is innate—it came into the world with you and it will leave with you, unless you continue to deny it and to act against it. Say to yourself many times: "I am good!" until you can feel the rightness of this. When you believe it, you will know it instinctively. You will become aware of your goodness and this is a very powerful awareness.

When you have completed these two steps you will be ready to heal yourself. This healing process often begins with anger at the perpetrator of the abuse. This anger is healthy and not to be avoided. You get to be angry—look at all you lost! You may need professional help to deal with this anger in a constructive way. You need to turn this anger outward, away from yourself, but you do not need to act on this anger directly to the perpetrator. You do not need to turn this anger into abusive behavior or you will be right back into your negative script. After the anger, forgiveness occurs. An understanding develops that your abuser was also following a destructive script. With forgiveness comes letting go.

The final step is becoming script free. You are responsible for your life. You are responsible for your own behaviors. If you continue to abuse yourself or others, now it is your fault because you know you have other choices. Up to now, you may have been caught in a pattern that was not of your making. Now you know differently and you are free to make your own choices. There is no good reason, ever, to abuse yourself. There is no need, ever, to punish yourself or to be destructive. You can love yourself, accept your dark side, forgive yourself for your mistakes, let go of your painful past and get on with the business of living life to the best of your abilities. If you choose to continue to hate yourself and to behave in destructive ways, recognize that now this is your choice and not the result of faulty training. Your inner child is now your victim. This child deserves to be loved, deserves to be treated well, deserves to be safe and secure. You are the only one who can compensate for the past. What better purpose do you have for your life?

I am doing so much and nothing's working—what's wrong?

This question is often asked by overachievers, obsessive-compulsive types, and perfectionists. These people become obsessed with *doing* and cannot understand why they feel so tired and so out of control. When we feel this way, we need to ask, "Who and what are we doing all this for?" Most likely, the answer is for others, for external rewards, for the Weak Ego. Doing is the focus of the western model; doing is not being. They are two completely separate things. Doing is not the same as being and doing it faster does not lead to being.

The Being Model is not contingent on doing. Granted, there are some things we can do to help us learn Self-Esteem. We can tell ourselves that we love ourselves, we can make choices and we can reward ourselves. These are doing activities. They help us to be but they are not the being. Remember, we do not have to *do* anything to be okay. Accepting ourselves, right now, as we are, is not doing something—it is being. Becoming aware of our centers requires the stopping of activity; it is the opposite of doing something.

This difference between doing and being can be one of the most difficult concepts to learn. We have been trained to do, to focus on activity, to achieve, to be productive. We have learned to value active behaviors and to devalue passive ones. We often refer to passive behaviors as "lazy" or "slothful." Activity looks like being in control, being productive, and our work ethic values these behaviors. Unfortunately, we cannot learn Self-Esteem and how to be by doing active behaviors. We cannot do Self-Esteem—we must be Self-Esteem.

The concept of paradox is helpful here. If you want something, you must let it go. Do less to get more. Slow down to develop the fastest outcome. The problem with doing is that it tends to focus on results—it quickly becomes goal-oriented, which is the western model again. Doing quickly becomes future-oriented. And that takes you out of the moment and out of yourself.

If you are doing too much, working too hard and always feeling tired, stop. Just stop! Relax, take three deep breaths and slow down. Refocus on yourself. Make yourself your first priority. Sleep more, meditate, do relaxation exercises, sit and be. The world really will not collapse if you take more time for yourself. You may have to reset your priorities, you may have to settle for less money and more balance in your life and you may have to give up some external rewards. It is your life and your choice. If you are racing through life, too tired to enjoy anything, what are you giving up?

Another interesting paradox is that we can achieve more when we are calmer, we feel more in control of ourselves when we are rested and life is more fun when we live in the moment. Being does not mean that we do not do anything. It does not mean that we have to retire to the nearest cave or mountaintop. Being means that we choose what we do and we do it well. It means that we take care of ourselves, we take "mental health time" to rest and recoup our energies and that we spend our energy on satisfying our own needs. This produces more energy that we can then choose to expend on others. We do both things we want to do and things we do not want to do and we know why we are doing them. Being means that we do not feel trapped, that life is not a rat race and that we can always find the time to fill our own needs.

What am I missing?

We ask this question when we realize that something is not working—we are feeling empty, incomplete, insecure, and unfulfilled. This question precedes the realization that the western Model of Doing (our training) is not enough. This question often means that we are in pain, we are confused and we do not know what else to do. We are ready for change and growth.

Life is difficult, painful, and full of problems. We have the ability to live amongst the pain and the problems and to feel peace and joy and a sense of belongingness. When we are centered, when we have Self-Esteem, we can see the many small miracles that make up life. When we are living the Weak Ego, we only feel the pain and become overwhelmed with the problems. We have the right, and the choice, to be accepted, to feel loved and to do the best we can, but we cannot expect life (the externals) to give us these rights. We must do the work by ourselves and for ourselves in order to achieve what we are missing.

Most of us tend to focus on the very things that we cannot control or change—the external things, the problems, the pain. We need to learn to refocus on what we can control and change. When we feel we are missing the joys of life, we usually feel resentful and hurt and we tend to look outward to have our needs met.

Learn to focus on what you can do and to let go of the need for others to do it for you. Begin by accepting that you are missing something. Focus on your own ability to take care of yourself. Instead of focusing on the problems, refocus on your own problem-solving abilities. You are an expert problem solver. Your past is composed of many problems that you have solved. You will solve your problems, one way or another. Choose how you want to solve them and do the best you can. Reward yourself for your efforts even if you do not get exactly what you want. Refocus from the pain of life to what this pain can teach you. Remember that pain is a part of life and it serves many purposes. It opens the door to change, it challenges your Self-Esteem and leads to even greater awareness of yourself. Pain is a great teacher if you are open to the lessons.

When you feel you are missing something, ask yourself if you are able to fill your needs. If you do not feel loved, focus on loving yourself. If you are not being recognized or rewarded, recognize and reward yourself. If you do not feel centered or peaceful, begin by accepting the place you are in and practice slowing down, taking care of yourself and loving yourself. Do for yourself what you are hoping others will do for you. Say to yourself what you would like to hear from others. Stop focusing on being happy or content and refocus on being aware. When you are desperate for something, you often drive it away from yourself. When you accept where you are and what you do have, the paradox often occurs, and you get what you want.

You have everything you need to take care of yourself as you are right now. If you are missing something that deals with your own feelings about yourself, you can change and get what you need. If you are missing something that is controlled by others or externals, you need to change your focus to what you can control. Ultimately, you cannot get what you really need from externals. Fulfill yourself and you will not feel that you are missing any part of this life.

Why do I feel that I am not here or anywhere?

People who have learned to be codependent, chronically depressed, insecure, or who have focused all their energies on the externals have spent years not being aware of themselves in relationship to their environments. For these people, it is a very familiar symptom not to feel a part of anything, not to feel belongingness anywhere and, in fact, to feel they just barely exist. By refusing to take care of ourselves, to put ourselves first and to know what we want and where we are, we are literally taking ourselves "out of the picture." Our feeling of not being here or anywhere is an accurate reflection of what we have done to our Self-Esteem. By not being centered and aware of ourselves in this world, we can easily lose sight of our centers and our awareness of the world.

It is a terrible feeling to go through the motions and not feel connected or a real part of what is going on. What is being described can be thought of as being psychologically lost. The solution is similar to what you do when you are physically lost—you ask for help, you ask someone to guide you to familiar territory, you get directions that you can follow. And then you act—you leave where you are lost and go to where you know. In the situation where you are psychologically lost, you must go to a place that you may not know—the center of yourself. In this case, you cannot find yourself by seeking a familiar environment. Often that is what causes you to live in the past—which is where you were before you felt lost. Or you may try to return to the last familiar place before you felt lost. You cannot go back to the past and you cannot recreate it and if you do succeed in returning to a familiar place, you may quickly find that it has changed and that the place cannot cure your feelings of being lost. There is only one cure and that is to discover yourself within yourself.

All paths lead to the center and this center can be found wherever you are. And once you have found your center, you will never be afraid of being psychologically lost again. You will know that you can feel belongingness wherever you may be because you feel it within yourself. Follow the steps outlined for developing Self-Esteem. Focus on the internals. Do not panic, go slowly and you will soon feel familiar with the process of discovering who and what you really are. The more you practice Self-Esteem, the more secure you become with yourself. The more centered you feel, the more aware you will be of your presence in the world. You will begin to know where you are at all times and you will feel that you belong even in unfamiliar settings. Your inner self will become your familiar and comfortable "home."

Why do I sometimes want to die?

Almost all of us, at sometime or other, have thought about dying as an escape from our pain or the reality of our lives. We want to die when we feel that we have lost control of ourselves or when we have given up control (depression). Sometimes we may think we want to die to punish others that we are angry with or to cause pain to others (revenge). At times, our negative feelings seem to overwhelm us and everything feels hopeless. We cannot see our way out of our negativity and we think that death may be the only escape. Wanting to die is the ultimate dis-couragement. It is the exact opposite of love of self.

Sometimes death feels like the easy way out and, if it feels like that, it probably is—the *easy way out*. It does not require courage to take the easy way; courage means taking the hard way and doing it when we do not understand or do not want to do it. The hero's task is to accept that there is pain, to accept that he or she cannot change the pain and to do the best he or she can anyway.

Wanting to die often means wanting to control something that is not in our control. We do not know the purpose of our lives and we do not know *why* we are here. We cannot know how our lives affect and interact with others and we cannot perceive the big picture. Dying before our time to die may be taking a shortcut and shortcuts frequently cause us to become lost and often take longer than the accepted path. Suicide may be the most dangerous gamble of all because we do not know what the next step is. Death is an ending but is it the ending of pain? Just as we take ourselves with us wherever we go, and we take our unresolved problems with us whenever we move, so too may we be taking the negativity and pain with us when we cause our own death.

Wanting to die and focusing our life energy on dying creates an illusion of powerfulness and control over things which are out of our power and control. We know that illusions prevent us from experiencing life. Longing for death as an escape from life is another way of focusing on the externals.

Death is not a negative thing when we do not try to control it. Death is part of the natural process of life and preparing for death as such means living our lives to the fullest *now*. In some ways all of life can be thought of as a rehearsal for death. If we live a good life, a loving and encouraging and enhancing life, then death, when it comes, will not be a difficult decision. In fact, it will not be our decision at all. The paradox here is that the more we live our lives to the best of our capabilities, the more like the hero we each try to be, the less fearful death will be. Developing strength and courage in this life means that we will take that same courage and strength with us when we die. When we accept the pain of our lives in the present, we become prepared to accept whatever happens in the future. Because we cannot know our purpose in this life, why not prepare for all eventualities?

If you are truly dis-couraged and thinking of taking the easy way out, seek encouragement. It is out there and you deserve to die in the best place you can be in. You deserve to die with dignity and grace and without fear of the unknown. You can only do this if you let go of your illusion of control. True courage means being uncertain and afraid and without comprehension of the whole but doing, living, anyway. You are facing a heroic task—your life— and you can be a hero to the only person that will go with you through this life—yourself.

Why do I feel so weak when I ask for help?

One of the great paradoxes of our time is that what looks like strength is really weakness and what appears to be weakness is really strength. This is particularly true when asking for help. It takes a lot of courage to admit that we do not know, that we are scared and lost. We have been trained to believe that we have to know and that it is wrong to be afraid. We have learned that showing feelings is a form of weakness. "Men don't cry, women don't show anger, and children should be seen and not heard." We are supposed to be strong, in control, and invincible. We are supposed to rise above our very humanness. Why? All the answers to this why are found in the Weak Ego. We want to look good for others; we want to appear to be something we are not; we want to fool the world. The problem is that in fooling the world, we fool ourselves. We lose sight of who we are and what we really want. It is so much simpler to be what we are, to feel what we feel, and not to be afraid of being weak at times. Paradoxically, when we admit our weaknesses we are showing our strengths, and when we deny our weaknesses we are exhibiting them.

Nobody can be perfect—everybody needs help at some time. Not recognizing this is a dangerous illusion. It is not an illusion but a sometimes painful reality that we are ultimately alone and must be responsible for changing ourselves but we do need guides to help us get on the path, support us, and sometimes encourage us to stay on the path to the center. It is not a weakness to know when we cannot do this alone. It is not a weakness to ask for help. It may be useful to think of our helpers as traffic police. They show us how to go, when to stop, and when to proceed safely, but they do not take us where we are going. They help us to avoid going down the wrong road and they give us directions when we are lost.

If you feel you need some help but you are afraid that you will appear weak when you ask for it, think of who is labeling you weak. If you are worried about the therapist's opinion of you, think again. All therapists need their clients. Their clients provide their reason for working and their clients are part of the therapist's own strength. Helping the client helps the therapist; every client teaches the therapist something. If you are concerned about others' opinions of you, remember that you cannot control what anyone else thinks or feels and that you are responsible only for yourself. The other person may think what they want but they cannot live your life for you. You must take care of yourself and let them take care of themselves. If you are worried that you feel weak when you ask for help, welcome this feeling as the beginning of fighting the Weak Ego. Admit that you feel weak but ask anyway. If you feel weak and do it anyway, you are being courageous. The hero does not always feel strong; moments of great courage are usually accompanied by feelings of inadequacy and weakness. And remember, weakness is not a feeling. It is a state of mind that you have learned and the model that you learned from is a weak model—weak in that it is faulty and does not produce balance, Self-Esteem, or a positive method for dealing with life.

Why do I feel so different from others?

The western model, the Doing Model, has taught us to be competitive. Our parenting and training have taught us to stress the differences between ourselves and others. We have learned to look at the roles, the facades, the status, money, clothes, education—all the outer trappings—of others versus ourselves and to feel either inferior or superior. When we use this model as our model for living, we perceive everyone else with judging eyes and judging eyes only attend to the differences between ourselves and others. When we have perceived the world this way for a long time, we lose sight of the similarities between ourselves and others and we cannot see the common ground that we share. Focusing on our differences rather than our similarities is a sure way of losing our sense of belongingness. And without belongingness we are truly lost and alone and miserable.

It is a great paradox that what others like about us, and what they relate with, is not our individual uniqueness—our differences from others—but our similarities with them. As humans, we share feelings and responses and the ability to understand and empathize with others. Our closeness comes from this shared awareness. We may not act in the same way to the same stimulus as someone else, but we do recognize the similarity of the feeling. We are unique in the way that we behave but we are similar in the way that we feel. All of us know pain even though each of us has our own reasons for our pain. We feel different from others when we fail to recognize the validity of another's pain. Being self-centered results in denying, ignoring, or failing to perceive the importance of others. Perceiving ourselves as different from others means being unable to relate to the humanness that we all share. It means being unable to see that we are all struggling to make sense of this crazy world and to be heroes. Feeling different from others and focusing on these differences results in loneliness. Most of us, when we are lonely, turn to others to take away the loneliness. We need others to fix us and this is one definition of self-centeredness. We need others but we do not value them because of their differences. We create the lonely trap—we say: "I need you but you cannot help me because you are different from me and you cannot possibly understand me because you have not done what I have done." Your uniqueness comes from your experiences—no one else has been through exactly what you have been through—and no one else has behaved exactly as you have behaved. Therefore, on one level, you are different from everyone else. But on another level, a higher level, you share your vulnerability and your feelings with others and this is what being similar means—sharing your humanness.

Group therapy is very powerful because it allows us to quickly see and share our similarities. What makes us feel may be different but the fact that we feel can be shared. We cannot share the exact experience but we can share the feelings that are generated. For example, no one else has my spouse but everyone can share my anger at my spouse because everyone is similar in their feelings of anger toward a family member. No one else made the exact mistakes that I made today but everyone can share the feeling of making mistakes. We can share our discouragements and our needs for encouragement. We can share our frustrations in our struggles to be the best we can be. We are similar in our goodness and in our need to do the best we can. We are similar in that we are all handicapped in our abilities to make sense of the world. We are similar in that we care, we want to "do good," and that we do not always know how to do this. We are similar in our frustrations and our confusion and our struggles. Recognizing these similarities creates belongingness which helps us in the process of Self-Esteem. Belongingness, recognizing our similarities, wanting to have relationships with others, are the reasons for developing Social Interest. This concept will be explained in the following section of this book.

IV. Relationship Issues

What is Social Interest?

Social Interest is a concept developed by Alfred Adler, which basically means the ways in which we relate with others. It follows after Self-Esteem, which is our relationship with ourselves. Social Interest flows from Self-Esteem in a natural manner because it is a human need to relate with others and to have relationships. This section of this book deliberately follows the previous sections which deal with developing Self-Esteem. This order is necessary because it is critical first to learn Self-Esteem and then to focus on relationship issues. The western model does not teach us to love ourselves first but jumps right into loving others. We cannot love someone else if we do not know how to love *ourselves*. And we cannot accept love from others if we do not realize that we are worthy of being loved. Once we love ourselves and recognize our worthiness to be loved, it is natural to practice Social Interest. We merely do to others what we have learned to do for ourselves. We accept, we support, we encourage, we forgive, we suspend judgments, and we let go when necessary. We cannot do any of these things with others until we can do them easily with ourselves.

In order to have Social Interest—healthy relationships with others—we must first have taken care of our own needs. Good relationships, "clean" relationships, cannot be comprised of needs and illusions and expectations. Social Interest is *not* about getting our own needs met through others nor is it about dependency and control issues. Social Interest is about being interested and accepting of where others are and being encouraging to others. It means caring, sharing, supporting, and understanding other people as they are and not interfering or trying to change them.

Being involved with others is one of our greatest challenges. Relationships are also one of our greatest joys. Most of us would not choose to learn Self-Esteem and then to become a hermit. Our preference is to have Self-Esteem and to live with others. This can often seem like a herculean task because we must learn the answers to the following questions: When do we take care of ourselves and when do we take care of others? How do we give of ourselves without becoming depleted? How do we take from others without becoming dependent upon them? What does a healthy relationship look like? When do we stick it out and when do we leave? How can we practice Self-Esteem when those around us have chosen not to or are not aware of what this means? Hopefully, the answers to these difficult questions will be found in the following pages.

What is a good relationship?

One way to think about relationships is to visualize a continuum:

| Narcissistic | | Codependent |
| (taking) | Healthy | (giving) |

Healthy relationships exist in the middle band of this continuum with flexibility to change and to move back and forth in the direction of the end points. Good relationships mean that no one involved in the relationship ever gets to the end point in either direction and no one stays in one place for very long. We all know what narcissists look like—these are the people who cannot give to others but who expect others to give everything to them. These people are the epitome of self-centeredness and usually have no intention of working on their own behalf when they can manipulate others to work for them. The codependent is the exact opposite and will be explained fully in the next question. This continuum shows that healthy relationships exist in the middle between too much giving and too much taking.

A good relationship is also comprised of mutual respect and kindness to the self and to the other. These are probably the two most important qualities of a good long-term relationship. These qualities can be, and often are, more critical to the relationship than love. If love means respect and kindness, then love is critical. However, too often what we define as love really means neediness and we treat the "ones we love" without respect and without kindness. If what we call love is really need masquerading as love, then it will not produce a good relationship. A good relationship is also comprised of trust, acceptance, communication, a genuine liking for the other person, and a willingness to compromise at times. There must be a recognition of the other as a separate person from ourselves, with his or her own needs and values and choices. There are things about each of us that are separate from the other person and separate from the relationship and this holds true for the other as well. Good relationships are not about constant closeness or consistent sharing and agreement. These attributes can quickly become suffocating and boring.

One important reason to have relationships is to challenge ourselves into growth and development. This growth and development cannot take place in a threatening or scary environment. Thus, a good, healthy relationship provides a safe, secure, encouraging place in this crazy world in which we can be ourselves without pretense. We are allowed to express feelings, make mistakes, experiment, take risks, and be nurtured along the way. In addition to providing support and nurturance, a good relationship also provides stimulation and sometimes a good "kick in the pants."

One of the problems today in having a good relationship is that there are very few long-term models available to emulate. Our society (the western model) has taught us that sexual attraction and addiction to the other are the critical components for our relationships. It has also taught us that the purpose for having a relationship is to get our needs met through the other. The only way to get past this training is to recognize that the first and most important relationship that you can have is the one that you have with yourself. All your other relationships will follow from that—you can never have a better relationship with someone else than you do with yourself. No one else can love you the way you want to be loved; no one else can fill your needs.

What is a codependent? How can I stop being one?

The term *codependent* developed from the field of substance abuse after counselors and clinicians became aware that the spouse of the addictive person was also sick from being overinvolved with the addict and the problem. Codependents become addicted to the helping or enabling role and frequently find this harder to give up than the addict giving up the addiction. A clear explanation of codependency is the following joke: On his or her deathbed, the codependent sees the other's life flash before his or her eyes.

Another way to understand the concept is that codependent means caring more for others then we do for ourselves and taking care of their needs (as presumed by us) more than we take care of our own needs. In order to do this, we must spend a lot of time dancing in others' heads in order to figure out what they are needing, what they are thinking and feeling and what will work to change them. All our energies are focused on changing others. The codependent lives in a world of illusion for the future; "if only____" becomes the goal for life. "If only the other will stop doing what he/she is doing, life will be wonderful. If only the other will change, then I will be okay." The sad fact is that even if the other does give up the addiction, does change, the codependent's life is still stuck in illusion and she or he does not know how to function without the enabling behaviors. It takes a lot of effort and work to change our focus from others onto ourselves. The codependent usually has no idea how to begin to refocus.

The tricky thing about codependency is that all of us have some codependent tendencies. All of us help others, sometimes to the exclusion of ourselves. It is easy to become involved in someone else's problems and it feels good to nurture and take care of others. The secret between being codependent and being caring is a matter of degree. There are times when we can put others' needs ahead of our own and times where we can give a great deal. But these times need to be short-term and not chronic. We need to know when we will stop and how we will take care of ourselves. We need to know that what we are doing is a gift and that we are doing it for ourselves and not to change the other person. (The only exception to this is the taking care of small children. We do this caretaking because they have a right to it. Children are vulnerable and helpless and depend on us for survival. We are not codependent when we are taking care of an infant or child. We may, however, become codependent with the adolescent. Part of caretaking means knowing when to let go and when to let the others do for themselves.)

If you think that you are codependent, that you have more than normal codependent tendencies, you will probably feel a lot of resentment and a lot of anger toward others. You will feel obsessed by your circumstances and unable to let go of the worrying, the caretaking, and the guilt. If you find that you are doing more worrying about someone else's life than your own life, get help. Join a support group, read the literature on codependents, find a counselor or therapist who understands codependency and begin to let go. The way to stop being co-dependent is to begin to be in-dependent. Practice focusing all that attention from the other person onto yourself. Take care of yourself first. Let them take care of themselves. If the other cannot take care of himself or herself, tell the person to get a professional. You are an amateur in the helping business and you are quitting. If you have to, let the other person go. You are not responsible for his or her life or addiction. You can only live your life!

Why can't I have a good relationship?

This question is frequently asked by those who are desperate for someone to love them and for someone to accept them as they are and to fill their needs. This is too much to ask of anyone else. The paradox here is that no one else can give us what we are not willing to give ourselves. If we love ourselves, accept who we are right now and fill our own needs, we will not be desperate for relationships and when we are not needy or desperate, good relationships occur. If we do these things, love ourselves and take care of our needs, we will not need to be in relationships. We will be okay with ourselves. If we are not okay with ourselves, we will be attracted to relationships that are destructive and others who are not okay with themselves will be attracted to us. It is almost as if we wear invisible-to-ourselves but visible-to-others neon signs on our foreheads which attract others with the same signs. If we have Self-Esteem, we attract others who also have it. If we do not love ourselves, we attract those who also do not love themselves.

Good relationships are comprised of healthy people. A relationship cannot make the people in it healthy. If you are looking for someone else to take care of you or make you happy, the person you will attract will most likely also be looking for someone to make him or her feel loved. The relationship that follows will not be healthy. Both of you will get caught in a vicious and destructive cycle of trying to get your own needs met by someone who is also very needy. Oftentimes, the only way out of the cycle is to end the relationship. And if you do not learn how to correct this by taking care of yourself before you begin a relationship, chances are that you will repeat the cycle over and over.

We have not been trained to know how to have good relationships. Unless we are very lucky, most of the relationships around us are dysfunctional and frequently destructive to the participants. Our movies, television, music, and fairy tales all foster the illusion and expectation that the perfect person will suddenly appear and we will fall madly in love and nothing else will matter. This fantasy of relationship is similar to an addiction in that someone else will take us out of the reality of our life and everything will get better. If we believe this fantasy, we will quickly discover that the price for the high is not worth the low. Bad relationships cost too much—they are emotionally draining and kill the spirit. All addictions, including relationship addictions, are against the self. They stop us from functioning to the best of our abilities and they detract us from the real business of life. They misuse our energies and they kill our creativity. Having no relationship is better than having a dysfunctional one. Besides, there is no such thing as no relationship because we are having a relationship with ourselves.

Focus on this one; it is the only one that you can control. It is the only one that results in change and that makes you balanced and centered. The only good reason to want a relationship with someone else is to share yourself with the other. If you begin the relationship by feeling less than worthy, less than deserving of love, how can you then expect the relationship to be better than what you are bringing into it? An analogy would be going into battle without weapons, without armor, without training, and expecting to win. Impossible! You are more than your relationships and your relationships can never provide more than what you are willing to do for yourself.

Why can't I fall in love with the "right" person?

Often in our relationships with others we mirror what is going on in our relationships with ourselves. If we are not secure with ourselves, we will fall in love with those who do not love us. If we do not believe that we are worthy of being loved, we will not be attracted to those who do love us. We are attracted to what we think we deserve. If we think we deserve to be punished (even at an unconscious level), we will find someone who is destructive to us. Whatever we really feel about ourselves will tend to be reflected by our relationships. If we feel positive and good about ourselves, we will have relationships with people who feel good about themselves and about us. If we are negative, our relationships will reflect the negativity. We do indeed reap what we sow.

Looking for the "right" person is a case in futility. There is no one right person, except you with yourself. Statistically, there are thousands of people that you are compatible with. The secret to finding them is to be compatible with yourself. Then, and only then, will healthy others appear. Stop having expectations about what the other person will look like and do for you. Instead, focus on what you look like, what you are, and what you will do for yourself. Stop looking. Enjoy your own company. Practice being okay without a relationship. It is never easier to learn Self-Esteem and to practice it then when you are alone. If you are used to taking care of yourself, to filling your own needs, then the challenge of being in a relationship will not be overwhelming. If you cannot take care of yourself when you are alone, it will be much more difficult to learn to take care of yourself when you are involved with someone else.

Most of us become aware of learning about Self-Esteem after we are in a relationship. While it is less complicated to practice Self-Esteem on our own, we do not have to leave the relationship in order to learn to take care of ourselves. But we do have to reprioritize what we will do for ourselves and what we will give up for the relationship. This does not have to be a negative thing for our relationships. Taking care of ourselves can be a positive thing in our relationships—we become good role models for others.

Loving yourself does not mean that everyone else will love you. Once you love yourself, it becomes easier to accept that others do not love you. Just as you yourself do not love everyone you know, others have the same right with you. Do not waste your time and energy on those who do not care about you. There are enough people around who do care for you to focus on. And if you feel that there is no one else who loves you, then you owe it to yourself to care more for yourself.

Relationships are about balance, not about rights and obligations. Relationships are about challenge and stimulation, not about comfort. Relationships are about expansion and growth, not about standing still or staying put. Rather, they are about allowing each other to change and letting go. The best relationships are those in which both people let each other be. We can love ourselves unconditionally and we can practice trying to love our partner unconditionally. We may never achieve this goal but we can learn from our efforts. If you want unconditional adoration, get a puppy. Your partner is not in the business of always adoring you. There is no one "right" partner for you but there are plenty of good people around to have healthy relationships with. But first, you must be healthy yourself so that you are ready for a good relationship with another.

What is the role of sex in the relationship?

This question is frequently asked by people who have "good" sex in a "bad" relationship or who have a "good" relationship with minimal to no sex. Nothing seems to be more confusing than sexual issues in relationships. Sex and money are the two issues that most couples disagree about. The western model teaches us that one of the most important qualities in the relationship is our sexual attraction to the other person. As most of us are painfully aware, what initially attracts us to the other is usually not sustainable over the long term and often repels us in the end. Sexual compatibility certainly adds a wonderful dimension to the relationship but sexual compatibility is not enough to sustain the relationship.

Andrew Greeley discusses sex as a gift from God, a way of playing and a rehearsal for unification, for becoming one with another and eventually with God. Good sex is one of life's great joys, one of the rewards for being and a marvelous release of stress and tension. It allows us to play, to share, and to be aware of ourselves and others in a natural, nonverbal dimension that is unique. Good sex heightens a good relationship. It cannot substitute for a dysfunctional one. Frequently, there is a confusion between sex and intimacy with sex providing the only means of closeness in the relationship. Sex accentuates intimacy; it does not provide it. It is an interesting phenomenon that many couples involved in dysfunctional relationships report having incredible, intense sex which adds to the confusion about their relationship. It is as if the bedroom is the only arena in which the couple can agree and feel connected. When this occurs, sex is being used as a substitute for all the missing variables in the relationship—communication, nurturance, acceptance, sharing, etc.

We are sexual beings; our sexuality is a natural attribute. Unfortunately, most of us have become conflicted and confused about our sexuality. This again is a result of our training and the bad press that sex is receiving in our culture. There has been too much emphasis on the use of our sexuality and of the sexual act itself in order to achieve other goals. We have been taught either to emphasize our sexuality to attract others or to hide it from others, as if being sexual is "bad" or "dirty." We have learned that men get to be more overtly sexual than women and sex is often used as a power and control issue. Because our sexuality is a natural part of our being, being comfortable with our sexuality is a natural process strongly related to our Self-Esteem. The more we love ourselves, the more comfortable we feel in our own bodies, the more accepting we become of what we physically look like, the more aware we are of our own sexuality and the less we fear it.

Good relationships, those that are composed of two healthy people, will not use sex as a contest. The persons in a good relationship will allow sex to be a natural part of the relationship and will not worry about frequency or always having phenomenal sex. Long-term couples know that sex is like any other part of the relationship—sometimes it works better than at other times. Almost all couples go through periods where sex seems to be less important than usual and they allow for this flexibility. There are periods in our lives in which we are more sexual and periods in which we are less. Often, these periods do not coincide with what is going on with our partner. Some compromise, acceptance, and understanding are necessary in order to keep sex in its proper perspective. If we cannot do these things in other areas of our lives, it will be impossible to be flexible and allow our sexual needs and desires to change across time.

Why can't I change my partner?

There are two prevalent and destructive illusions that many of us believe when we enter into relationships: 1) that the person we are with will change by virtue of being with us—we will help him/her to change and 2) that the other person will never change at all and remain exactly as he/she is in the beginning. Both of these are illusions because they have no basis in reality. People are continually changing; no one can escape the process of change. However, no one can change anyone else. We can change ourselves, we can make new choices and reprioritize our values but we can never predict what our partners will choose to change. The most we can do is to provide role models for our significant others and to encourage them in their efforts. We can try to provide a safe environment conducive to change but none of the above guarantee that the other will change in the manner that we would choose for them.

Being powerful enough to change others is the fallacy of codependents and often small children. "If only I am good enough, do the right things, push the right buttons, the other will change." But the others do not change unless they choose to change. They will not change when the responsibility or need for the change is not their own need or responsibility. Children and codependents have no responsibility (i.e., control) over the other's behaviors, but by taking on this responsibility, they actually prevent the change from occurring. We only have control over changing ourselves. Wanting someone else to change will not make their change occur. Investing all our efforts into the change process of another only makes us sick and robs us of our own Self-Esteem.

Demanding, cajoling, manipulating, threatening, ordering, begging, and bargaining for the other to change only produces a discouraging and destructive environment. When we are engaged in all this negativity, we are changing ourselves—for the worst. We are doing less than the best for ourselves and we are engaged in behaviors that are not conducive to our own Self-Esteem. The irony here is that the partner usually continues to do whatever he/she wants to do but now feels justified in blaming us for producing so much negativity and such a destructive environment.

Do not get caught up in the amateur therapy trap. Even if, or especially if, your partner is asking you to be the change agent, do not do it. Professionals in the field quickly learn not to be their family's therapist. Only amateurs believe that they can be therapists for their close relations. You cannot be objective about those that you are involved with. It is impossible to provide consistent unconditional acceptance to someone who is intimately connected with your own quality of life. It is difficult to put yourself in an expert position and also maintain equality and balance in the relationship. If you are asked to be the change helper, the best you can do is support and encourage the other to seek expert help.

Again, take care of yourself first. Take responsibility for your life. Do what you have to do to insure that your life is the best it can be. This sounds deceptively simple, but it is not easy. Focus your needs for change on what you can change—what you can control—you yourself. Practice acceptance, first toward yourself and then toward your partner. If you absolutely cannot accept your partner as is and if he/she shows no inclination to want to work on change, then make some choices. Leave if necessary. Remember, it is your choice to be in this relationship.

If I change, will my partner?

There are three answers to this question: yes, no, and maybe. The *yes* means that when one part of a system—the relationship—changes, the whole system is affected and changes do occur. The *no* means that we cannot control the changes except for ourselves. Changing ourselves will not insure changes in others; we may change the way in which we perceive others and we may change in that it becomes easier to accept others. The *maybe* means that some changes may occur but they may not be the ones we wanted and they may not be in the desired direction.

The motivation for changing ourselves cannot be to change the other. If this is the case, then we are involved in manipulative and bargaining behaviors and not with true change. Changing ourselves is hard work and requires strong desires for the changes and commitment to the process of change. When we enter into this commitment with ulterior motives (changing others) and we do not gain the desired results, we may find ourselves right back in the codependent cycle: we are doing all the work, taking all the responsibility, and the reasons for our efforts are not occurring. Chances are, we will begin to feel resentful and cheated and angry at the person who is not changing. We may also feel angry with ourselves. All of these are destructive to the development of our own Self-Esteem, and our efforts will backfire.

If you choose to change, do it for one reason only—because you want to change for yourself. Then the change is in your control. Remember, you can only control the way you choose to feel about yourself and your behaviors based on your feelings. Nothing else is in your control. The way others react to your change is totally out of your control. Logically, you may believe that if you change in a positive direction, your close relationships will also improve in a positive manner. Unfortunately, relationships are not logical and sometimes the opposite occurs. The relationship begins to fall apart or the others around you become more dysfunctional. This is a common reaction, well known to family therapists and systems experts. Sometimes the deterioration of the system is short-term and the family stabilizes and becomes more functional once they get used to the change. But sometimes the opposite occurs and the relationship cannot cope with the change. This is one reason why it is critical to change for yourself, change because you have to, no matter what the consequences. This does not mean that all changes are going to put the relationship at risk. Many changes occur which clearly enhance the relationship. However, the more dysfunctional the relationship, the more likely that it will not adapt to the change. These relationships are already at risk and creating great pain for those involved in them. If your relationship is so tenuous that changing yourself for the better will destroy the relationship, then you may need to consider how valuable this relationship is to you and your quality of life.

If you are trying to change so that someone else will change, you are absolving them of their responsibility to change and you are taking the credit for any changes which may occur. When you change yourself, you get all the credit for the change because you did it. You did the work, you felt the pain, you stuck it out, and you achieved what you wanted to. Everyone else has the same rights—they get all the credit for their changes. You did not do it for them; they did it for themselves. Do not try to choose change for others—it never works!

What can I do for others?

The very best thing that anyone can do for others is to be a good role model of Self-Esteem and Social Interest. There are not nearly enough healthy role models in this crazy world. By loving yourself, taking care of your needs, and practicing Self-Esteem, you will be providing a visible, balanced, and positive model for others if they choose to change. By practicing acceptance, lack of guilt, encouragement, taking responsibility for yourself, and being centered, you will be demonstrating that this is possible and you will be teaching others by your example. This is the most powerful type of teaching even though often we are not aware of what we are modeling for others. Much of practicing Self-Esteem involves nonverbal behaviors and these can only be learned from demonstration. The paradox here is that the more you do it for yourself, the more powerful a model to others you are. The old saying "Practice what you preach" is relevant here but in this example, you do not need to preach. Just practicing is enough.

If you can accept yourself and stop trying to be perfect, then you can accept others with their imperfections. This acceptance is very powerful and allows others to begin to accept themselves. If you can forgive yourself for your mistakes and learn from them, others around you will perceive that there is a choice in how they treat their own mistakes. They may not choose to learn from you but they will not be able to use the old justification: "Everybody else is trying to be perfect." When you let go of guilt and self-punishment, you model the possibility that these are not necessary. Every time that you say "No" to someone, you are giving them the right to say "No" to you. If you can say "No" without guilt, you are giving them the permission to do so. By taking care of your own needs, you are allowing others to take care of their needs. When you take risks, others are more apt to take risks. And so it goes. We are affected by those around us. We do respond to encouragement and support and we do react to the negativity and discouragement in the world. We need a lot more of the positive to counteract the negative. You can be a positive force in your world.

One of the most powerful things that we can model for others is unconditional love. When we have Self-Esteem and practice unconditional love for ourselves, we model this by our very being. We do not have to *do* anything; we are demonstrating by being. By allowing ourselves to *be*, we allow others to be. By not externalizing and blaming, we stop the blame-game. All of these provide a safe place for others and people desperately need safe places.

Social Interest does not force change upon others. Rather, it allows change to occur and encourages positive change. Social Interest, the extension of Self-Esteem toward others, fosters growth and development. We need others to teach and to learn from—we need others to interact with—to share the discovery of ourselves—to rejoice with them in their discoveries. We need others because we are all connected, united, and part of the same whole. We can grow together toward reunification. We cannot do this by ourselves. We also need others for the challenge of overcoming our separateness in the world; we need to discover our belongingness and to share our similarities. We need others as they need us—not to take care of but to be caring with; not to do things for but to do things together. In short, the best we can be for others is exactly the same as the best we can be to ourselves.

What is wrong with putting others first?

The popular name for the behaviors involved in putting others ahead of ourselves is "people-pleasing." This term accurately describes what we are doing when we elevate the needs of others above our own needs. If indeed we do need others, what is wrong with sacrificing ourselves to them? Why can't we please others and try to make them happy? The answer to these questions is again a matter of degree. Sometimes we can choose to sacrifice what we want or need for someone else. Sometimes we can try to please others. The key word here is *sometimes*—but not all the time. Most people-pleasers are involved in the chronic activities of taking care of others. They have never learned to do the same activities for themselves and they wait and hope for others to please them. This is the danger of putting others first consistently.

Our western model (and most religions) have taught us, "Do unto others as you would have them do unto you." The focus is nearly always on the "Do unto others" part and rarely on the second half of this saying. How do we know what we would want them to do for us if we are not aware of our own needs and wants? And if they did unto us, could we accept it and be worthy of their gift? Most people-pleasers have focused all their energy on giving out and have no awareness of what they want or need for themselves. They are hoping that someone else will read their minds and know what is the right thing to do for them. People-pleasers give to get back and their presents always have strings attached. These unclean givers often presume that they know what the other person needs better than that person knows. Thus, they give unwanted or unnecessary gifts. The results from all this people-pleasing are resentments, hurts, and misunderstandings. These are not at all the intention of "doing unto others."

People-pleasing is a modern term for martyring. Most of us are not cut out for sainthood. And a martyr can be very difficult to live with. Paradoxically, the true saints gave because they wanted to give. They gave ultimately for themselves. They were practicing Self-Esteem at a higher dimension; they fulfilled their own desires and moved out of worldly concerns. Most saints were not aware of nor concerned with their saintliness. They were following a higher calling. People-pleasing, putting others first, is the opposite of saintliness. People-pleasers are all too aware of what they are doing and they are doing it in a self-centered manner. They are giving in order to get their own needs met by others. By putting others first, they are hoping to get love, respect, adoration, security, acceptance, etc., back from those they are giving to. None of these things can be bartered or bought. By putting others first, people-pleasers are relinquishing their own rights and responsibilities along with the gifts they give.

Putting others first is a present you give to them. As with all presents, it is only meaningful if you, the giver, want to give the gift with no ulterior motives. This is the only good reason to give a present. It is of no consequence what the receiver does with the gift. The reason for giving is to bring joy to you, the giver. And that is enough. Taking care of others is a very large gift to give. Only do it when you are sure that there are no strings attached. (Again, the exception is small children. Take care of them even when you do not want to. They are not responsible for being in your care. They have no other options and cannot take care of themselves. Another exception would be others who are dependent on you due to illness or handicapping conditions, although there may be other options available for their care. Animals also are vulnerable to the people who own them.) The only way that you can give gifts without strings is to first take care of your own needs. In order to do this, you must put yourself first. You must recognize what you need and want and you must do the work to meet your own needs. You cannot take care of yourself and also people-please at the same time. Besides, once you are taking care of yourself, you will find your need to please others will disappear. When you like yourself, you will want others to like you for what you are and not for what you do for them. By satisfying your own needs, your ulterior motives for giving will no longer be important.

Perhaps all of this will be more clear if we turn the saying around—"Do unto yourself as you would have others do unto you." This is the essence of learning Self-Esteem. Once you do this, the paradox occurs and it is easier to "Do unto others as you would have them do unto you." This is the essence of Social Interest. You can only practice Social Interest *after* you have learned to practice Self-Esteem. This is what the western model has failed to teach us. This concept is at the heart of all religions. Know that you have worth, that you are good, and that you deserve to be loved. Learn forgiveness, acceptance, and letting go. You will benefit and the others around you will benefit. Only put others first temporarily; in the long term put yourself first. You are worth your own attention. You can please yourself.

How will I know when to give to others and when to say "No"?

First of all, make sure the other person wants what you are giving. Do not presume that they need your services and do not give to others when you yourself are needy. The whole thing will backfire. Avoid needing to be needed. This is another trap that is easy to fall into. Make sure that the gift you are giving—your time, energy, services, sacrifice—is clean and that there are no ulterior motives on your part. If you are asked to give when you do not want to do so but feel you must, make sure it is a short-term situation so that you know from the beginning exactly what you are getting into and when you will stop. If you cannot do these things, it is better in the long run not to give of yourself. If you find that you are involved in a situation where you are giving too much and becoming resentful or angry, stop giving. No gift to another is worth destroying yourself. There is no law that states that once you begin giving you must keep on giving. Beware of people who expect you to always be the giver. They are lacking Self-Esteem and will not encourage you to take care of yourself.

The following story is a clear example of the danger of giving too much. In a dense forest lives a swamp that is always depressed and gloomy and unhappy with his lot in life. One sunny day a brand-new tractor rolls off the assembly line and takes a walk in the forest where the swamp lives. The tractor is whistling and singing and delighted to be alive when he comes across the swamp. "Good morning," he says to the swamp. "Isn't this a wonderful day!" "Hmph," replies the swamp. "What is so good about it? Here I am stuck in this shady part of the forest where the sun never shines through the trees and I'm tired of being an old gloopey swamp." "I wish I could help you," says the innocent tractor. "Is there anything I can do?" The swamp is thoughtful. "Well, if you *really* want to help, I suppose you could shovel some dirt into me and then I would dry up and stop being a swamp." "What a good idea," says the tractor. "I'll be happy to help you stop being a swamp." And the enthusiastic tractor energetically begins shoveling dirt into the swamp. This goes on for a couple of hours with little result to the status of the swamp. The swamp begins to grumble: "I don't think that you are shoveling fast enough to make a difference." "Okay," replies the tractor, "I'll shovel even faster." The day wears on and the little tractor is getting very tired. The swamp looks exactly as it looked in the morning. Now the swamp starts getting mad at the tractor. "If you really cared about me, there would be some results. I don't think your heart is really into helping me." By now the tractor has invested the whole day in trying to help the swamp and he really feels committed to his role to try and change the swamp. So he speeds up his efforts even though he is feeling weak and exhausted. He shovels dirt while the swamp sleeps throughout the night and he continues to work the next day while the swamp grumbles and complains about his poor effort and his lack of *real* caring. The tractor literally works himself to death and slowly sinks into the wet, muddy swamp. There is no evidence that the tractor has ever been there at all. The swamp remains a swamp and waits for the next tractor to come along and save him from himself.

What could the tractor have done? If he had learned Self-Esteem —how to take care of himself—he might have asked the swamp what the swamp was willing to do to change. Or he might have passed by the swamp and recognized that this was a dangerous trap. Or being a tractor with Social Interest, he might have offered to help the swamp for a little while. Then when he realized that his help was not working, he might have gone on his way feeling good about his efforts even though the swamp was still a swamp. In all cases, had the tractor learned Self-Esteem, he would never have given his life to the swamp.

Some people are natural tractors (givers) and they are attracted to those who are swamps (takers). In order to change the ending to a happy one, both the swamps and the tractors of the world need to learn to take care of themselves. The swamps of the world need to learn to do for themselves and the tractors need to learn to let the swamps help themselves. The tractors allow the swamps to continue being swamps. By giving so much, the giver puts the taker in a one-down position, a victim role, and victims tend to resent and hate their so-called saviors. It is easy to perceive the destructiveness of the takers but there is also destructiveness in too much giving. The goal of the givers, feeling good and taking credit for the outcome, can be a larger goal than the one that the taker wants.

Remember the cookie jar theory: bake cookies for yourself first and then bake cookies for others. Give when you are full and you will not feel depleted from the act of giving. You can sacrifice yourself for others as long as it does not feel as though you are sacrificing anything. As soon as you feel the sacrifice, stop giving and take care of your own needs.

What is a "dysfunctional family"?

This term is currently used to define families or relationships that do not function in a healthy manner. People involved in these families are caught in some type of vicious cycle that is causing all concerned pain and destructive patterns of relating with each other and to themselves. Families with an alcoholic, a drug addict, a member with a personality disorder, an abusive member, a criminal, or any type of destructive person are usually dysfunctional. This term evolved from perceiving the family as a system rather than focusing only on the offender's problem. When one person in the family has a major problem, the whole family has the problem and everyone becomes involved in the mess. Dysfunction can also occur without an offending person—if there is a big family secret or outside conflict that affects the family in a destructive manner, the family can become dysfunctional. Everyone in the family becomes a victim in some way of the problem.

Unfortunately, too many families today seem to be dysfunctional. These families have too much tension, a lack of meaningful communication, an inability to deal with feelings, a lack of support for each other, unnecessary and destructive criticism, a discouraging atmosphere, and the inability for each member to develop and grow in a positive way. The home feels more like a war zone than a safe, secure place. A sure sign that we live in a dysfunctional family is when we hate or are afraid to go home. Frequently, we find splitting among the family members, tenuous alliances, many secrets, and a great deal of back stabbing. Each member of the family learns unhealthy defenses in order to survive, and the children of these families take this faulty training with them into their relationships. In this way several dysfunctional families will evolve out of one dysfunctional family of origin. Dysfunctional families produce dysfunctional people who then go on to create dysfunctional families.

Family therapists discovered that it is not enough to take the person with the problem out of the family for treatment and then to send the "patient" back into the dysfunctional system. In order to have positive change, the emphasis must shift to the family unit and away from the designated problem person. At times even concerned parties outside of the immediate family—close friends, other relatives, helpers who have become involved with the problem—must also be involved in the treatment intervention in order for change to occur. Frequently a crisis is needed in the family in order to get everyone involved in treatment. The paradox of crisis is that it can often be the most positive event for a dysfunctional family if the crisis precipitates the change process.

Most dysfunctional families do not change because to remain dysfunctional is easier and more familiar than to risk the unknown. The familiarity of the problem and the family's responses to it create a crazy kind of security for the family members. "Better the devil you know than the one you don't know." It seems easier to remain static and stuck than to learn and develop new patterns. This is a terrible illusion because dysfunctional relationships require much more energy to maintain than healthy ones and the effort involved in this maintenance does not produce positive rewards for anyone involved. If the family refuses to change its destructive system, then the family member who wants to change must choose to do so on his or her own regardless of the family's reaction. This can be a very difficult choice, sometimes leading to separation from the sick system. However, we are responsible to ourselves first!

Why am I still afraid of my mother or father?

There are a surprising number of adults who ask this question. These are people who grew up in dysfunctional families and who were abused or intimidated by one or both of their parents. This fear may continue into their adult lives in spite of separation from the parents, including death of the feared parent, and despite their present status in the world. People who are not afraid of anything else or who are professionally "successful" may still harbor anxiety and supposedly irrational fears when they think of or encounter this parent. Often, these people revert to a childish state and act in immature ways when confronted by this parent. Large, powerful men and strong women quake when they have to deal with this feared individual, even if the parent is old, sick, weak, and frail. Why?

This reaction is easier to understand if we are familiar with the concept of the inner child. Remember, this inner child does not "grow up" and is involved with our early feelings and reactions. When we are still afraid of our parent, it means that we are perceiving this parent through the eyes of the inner child. We are perceiving this parent as a powerful, needed person that we are dependent upon for our survival. Because they inflicted so much pain upon us when we were little, we still view them as stronger than we are and able to hurt us. It made sense to be afraid of them when we were little but it no longer makes sense to fear them now that we are able to survive without them. However, the inner child does not relate to this type of rational logic. You cannot reason with a fearful child; you must understand and relate to the feeling.

Once you learn to parent your inner child, then you can see your hurtful parent with your adult eyes. You can begin to see his or her insecurities and needs and weaknesses. You will then see through his or her so-called power over you and you can let go of the control that he or she is exerting over you because of your fear. You will view this parent as a person in the world rather than an object of pain. If you can separate yourself from this parent, you will see the evil in the abuse and you can choose not to participate in the abuse. You can get out of the victim role. Do not try to change your parent or have him or her acknowledge or apologize for the evil that has been done to you. This parent may not ever choose to do so and you may produce more pain for yourself. Instead, change yourself. Parent your inner child and give your child the support, encouragement, and security that you needed from your parent but never received. Do for yourself what this parent could not or would not do for you when you were a child. If your parent is still abusing you, get out of this sick system. Practice Self-Esteem and stay away from discouraging others. Make yourself strong and secure and loved and change your dependence to in-dependence. Give yourself what you need and want so that you need and want *nothing* from this parent. Only when you are free of fear and clean from neediness can you risk interaction with him or her. Do not try confrontation unless you have support. Do not try to be a therapist or a teacher for your parent. Remember, you can be angry and deal with this anger constructively without dealing directly with your parent. You have the right to be angry at your parent but you have an even bigger responsibility to yourself—to take care of yourself, let go of your past fears and get on with your own life. Once you no longer need your parent for survival, you no longer need to be dependent. Your inner child now has you to parent it. You can be fearless!

Why do I hate?

Hatred can be conceived of as unresolved anger, unfulfilled needs, and unacknowledged pain which have been externalized onto another person or situation or internalized into ourselves. We tend to hate people who harm us or withhold what we want or need. We hate people who victimize us. When we are victims, we hate ourselves for being weak and powerless. We hate the concept of unfairness because it makes us feel hopeless and out of control. We hate the fact that we cannot be perfect and we hate our vulnerability in the world. We begin by hating others and we end by hating ourselves. The problem with hating is that it is pervasive and creates a vicious and self-destructive cycle. It is the opposite of acceptance. No matter how deserved the hatred may be toward someone else, our hatred is part of ourselves and eventually turns against us and destroys our own spirit and Self-Esteem. It is very difficult to love ourselves unconditionally when there is hatred inside of ourselves. Hatred is like the rotten apple in the barrel; unless the rot is removed, it spreads to all the good apples.

The best way to deal with hatred is to resolve the anger, fulfill the needs, and acknowledge the pain. Accept that you hate and work on letting go of this hatred. Do not waste your time and energy in justifying why you hate or in denying that you do hate and do not look for support of your hatred because you will probably find it. Hating something or someone will never change the thing or the other but it will change you in a destructive way. Stop focusing on the thing that you hate and refocus on yourself. Look for the other feelings that comprise the hatred; become aware of the sadness and the anger and the fear that are involved in your hating. Acknowledge these feelings but do not try to control them. Remember, you cannot control your feelings but you can control how you express them or act on them. If you feel sadness in your hatred, cry, grieve what you are missing and let the pain pass. It will, once you have dealt with it. Do the same with anger—yell, jump up and down, beat up your pillow, write angry letters that you will never mail, share your anger with some neutral and supportive person who encourages you to feel without acting rashly upon your feelings. Anger, like all your other feelings, will pass if you acknowledge it and let it go. It will become impossible to hate if you no longer feel anger or sadness or fear or neediness. What is left to hate when you have taken care of your feelings and needs? If you hate someone because of the way that person is in the world, then you are involved in judging behaviors. You are saying that you are right and the other is wrong, you are good and he or she is bad, you know and the other does not.

The western model is based on boundaries, perceived values, and criticism. It holds the assumption that we can achieve perfection and that we are in competition with others. The eastern model, the Being Model, makes no assumptions. It is a model of acceptance. We are what we are and everyone else is what they are. We are only responsible for ourselves and when we hate, we are responsible for our hatred. We cannot control anything except ourselves but we can choose to stop hating. Others will not change whether we hate them or not. There will always be pain and injustice and unfairness in the world. Our hating will only add more negativity to a world which is already overloaded with destruction. Our acceptance and lack of hating may not change all the negativity but it will change our own. We may not be able to clean up the cesspool but we do not have to add to it. We can let go of the hating—it does no good.

What can I do when others hate me?

This question is in many ways the converse of the previous one. There are some similarities with the previous answer. Others hate us when we hurt them, withhold something they need or want from them, inflict pain upon them, and victimize them. People tend to hate us when they perceive us as evil or ignorant or sick. Frequently people hate us for the weakness that we show and they fear within themselves or they hate us for our strengths which they feel they lack. Sometimes people hate us for no apparent reason.

There is one major difference between hating and being hated. We can learn from being hated. We can use the fact that we are hated to produce change in ourselves and we can become aware of our behaviors and their effects upon others by focusing on why we are hated. If we accept the fact that we are hated, then we can consider what we want to do about this hatred. We can ask ourselves how we feel about ourselves and whether or not we feel that we deserve this reaction from them. If we can acknowledge and accept that we are doing harm to someone else, then we can choose to change our behaviors. We can begin to recognize our own insecurities that are driving us to the illusions of having power and control over others. We can learn why we feel the need to place others in a one-down or victim position. We can begin to understand why we are being discouraging and destructive. Once we can objectively accept that what we are doing is harmful, than we can choose to change. We cannot begin the change process when we are involved in denial, defenses, justifications, and externalizations. We can indeed learn more from our enemies than we do from our friends. We can let our enemies, those who hate us, become our teachers and our challenges to positive growth.

Suppose that we focus on our behaviors and we feel good about what we are doing and do not recognize the need for change. In this case we feel that we do not deserve the hatred and there is nothing we can learn from it. Again, accepting that we are okay and that the world is not fair will help us deal with the injustice of being hated. Just as we have the choice and responsibility for our own hatred, so do others. If we are really doing the best we can and not deliberately trying to cause harm or to victimize someone else and if our consciences are clear, then we do not have to spend our time and energy worrying about others' hatred. It really is their problem and responsibility to deal with and we do not want to become victims to those who perceive themselves as our victims. This will create a lose-lose cycle for everyone.

Self-Esteem means dealing with the reality that we cause pain to others. We cannot fill others' needs and we cannot take care of them in ways that they would like us to. We cannot take responsibility for them (unless they are the exceptions: small children, the sick and handicapped, animals, and the real victims of the world). People who lack Self-Esteem will often hate us for not engaging in the Weak Ego with them. We can accept this and let it go. We cannot become people-pleasers because we are afraid of being hated. Paradoxically, people-pleasers are more hated than those who practice Self-Esteem. The hatred belongs to the person who feels it. The best we can do is to trust ourselves, check our consciences and how we feel about ourselves, change our destructive patterns toward others as much as we can, and let go of their hatred. We can learn to be loving, first to ourselves and then toward others and, in this way, we will generate less hatred and more love in the world.

When do I know that it is time to leave the relationship?

The word *dysfunction*, when used in the relationship context, literally means that the relationship is not working—not functioning in a healthy manner. There are large degrees of difference among dysfunctional relationships. Sometimes a relationship that is stale or boring may feel dysfunctional. External stressors can also feel dysfunctional when they create unusual or unfamiliar patterns of behavior. Almost all relationships go through periods of being less functional than usual. These normal patterns in most relationships need to be contrasted with the severely dysfunctional relationships. The latter are the ones which involve abuse, addiction, physical or emotional destructiveness or harm to the involved members. When the potential for abuse or serious harm is high, the victim needs to leave the relationship as quickly as possible. We cannot take care of ourselves emotionally until we are assured of physical safety. We cannot work on change and growth when our energies are being consumed with basic survival needs. We have the right and we owe it to ourselves to put ourselves in safe environments if we have the slightest possibility of doing so. We do not have to choose to stay in a victim role if there is any way out.

Emotional safety is as important as physical safety. You cannot function to the best of your abilities if you are being emotionally abused. If you are involved with someone emotionally destructive to you, stop trying to change him or her and leave. If you are living with an alcoholic or an addict who expresses no interest in working on changing, you are better off leaving this person with their addiction rather than trying to deal with it. Remember, the addict's first concern is toward what he or she is addicted to. You cannot come before the addiction until the addict is willing to give it up. The success of an intervention process—"tough love"—with a dysfunctional family always involves the fact that the addict must choose between the addiction and the partner or family members. The addict cannot have both at the same time. No matter how painful the leaving may be, in the long run there will be less pain than staying in a hopeless situation. You have the responsibility toward yourself and your vulnerable children to remove yourselves from an abusive environment. Remember, safety ranks as the primary need for humans and animals. It is more basic than sleep or food or sex. Do not allow yourself to remain in an unsafe environment if there is any means of escape. You do not deserve to be in danger.

What about the other relationships—the ones where there is no danger but they are not functioning well? What about being bored or unhappy with the relationship? How do you know if and when to leave in these cases? A good rule here is to make no quick or rash decisions. Take some time and get some help. Think about the things that you feel are missing from the relationship and work on the ones that you can take care of by yourself. If you lack Self-Esteem, you may be placing unreasonable demands upon your partner and the relationship. If you have illusions and unrealistic expectations about what the relationship can do for you, you need to focus on these and change them. Do not leave a relationship because you are bored or unhappy without trying to change yourself. No relationship can always make you happy or stimulated. No relationship can do for you what you are not willing to do for yourself first. If you do leave, and do not work on your own Self-Esteem, you will just take all the garbage with you and it will cause rot in your succeeding relationships. Remember that Self-Esteem is not a relationship issue but an individual decision. You learn and practice Self-Esteem for yourself *before* you practice Social Interest. The relationship cannot make you healthy; you can only make yourself healthy.

Too many relationships fail unnecessarily because one or both partners are involved in the Weak Ego and expect their needs to be met from externals. These people will relationship-hop until they die or learn that they must give themselves what they are looking for. Then there are those that stay in unhealthy relationships far too long. These are usually codependents who are caught up in the "I can change the other" cycle. These people do not identify themselves as the problem but become consumed with the other. They need to be needed, to people-please, and to caretake. Again, they are looking for something outside of themselves to change.

Remember, you cannot control anything outside of yourself and you cannot change anyone but yourself. If you cannot learn and practice Self-Esteem in the relationship, leave the relationship. If, for any reason that is out of your control, you cannot be who you are in a relationship, leave the relationship. Try to leave without blame and recognize your own part in the sick cycle and take care of yourself. Do not make yourself a hostage to a sick relationship.

You stay in a relationship that you are physically and emotionally safe in and that allows you to change and work on yourself. You stay when you can work on your own needs and wants and the relationship allows you these freedoms. You stay in relationships that are going through tough times that are short-term or that are not due to the relationship itself. You stay when you can see that change is possible, not unrealistic. You stay until you know that you have done the best you can do and the relationship remains dysfunctional. In other words, you stay until you can leave with a clear conscience—you can leave and still feel good about yourself. You stay until you can leave with love.

How can I fall out of love?

We have left a relationship but we are still in love with our partner or we have been rejected by someone we love. How do we get over this relationship? Most of us have experienced being in love with someone who does not love us; most of us know what it is to be unable to have a relationship with the person we love. We know how incredibly painful it is not to be able to love and be loved. We cannot believe that anyone else has ever felt so much pain and still survived. We cannot imagine what it will feel like to be out of this pain and to stop loving the other person. It is important to know that it *is* possible to fall out of love and that we do have some control over this process. While we cannot control our feelings, we can control our obsession with the other and we can control our needs for the other. It is ironical that we often feel more pain leaving dysfunctional and unhealthy relationships than we do leaving healthy ones. That is because unhealthy relationships are about needs rather than about real love. The more needs that we have for the other, the more difficult it feels to give them up. We feel as if we are giving up a large part of ourselves rather than just the other person. This kind of relationship is called a *symbiotic* relationship because we cannot tell where we end and the other begins. It is as if we have been glued to the other person and now that we are unglued, we no longer feel complete. Being out of this type of relationship is a blessing in disguise because now we will be forced to glue ourselves back together and perceive ourselves as separate from others, complete and whole and independent. We do not need to thwart this process by glomming onto the next person who comes along or we will only be delaying our self-unification and adding more pain to our life.

Begin the process of falling out of love by accepting the fact that you need to be out of love with the other. Recognize that this will take time and will not happen overnight. It takes time to really love somebody else and it takes time to stop loving them. Change your focus from how much you love the other to how much you needed the other and then begin filling these needs for yourself. If you needed the other to feel loved, practice loving yourself. Act as if you love yourself and engage in loving activities toward yourself. If you needed the sex, masturbate and fantasize about others, not the loved one. If you needed the touch, get a massage or a facial or ask your friends and family for lots of hugs. If you needed the companionship, reach out to your friends, make new friends, extend yourself and begin new hobbies and activities. In the beginning all of these things will feel like poor substitutes for the person you are missing but, over time, they will compensate. Allow yourself to grieve and give yourself permission to really grieve for a certain amount of time every day. Set aside a grieving hour and hurt like hell for that hour and then force yourself to stop by getting involved in something else. Write letters that you will never send expressing your anger and sadness at your loss. Call a variety of people for support when you need it but avoid using one or two people consistently for support and a shoulder to cry on. In this way you will not abuse their friendship and not risk losing other important people in your life. Know that today and tomorrow will be horrible but next week will only be bad and a month from now it will start to be better. Pay attention to and value the moments that you are not in pain because they will be there amongst all the painful ones. In this way, you will have less tendency to get stuck in the pain. Focus on anything positive that is happening to you—sometimes we lose excess weight or need to sleep less or have more energy—and use these positives to work for you. You might as well be miserable and doing something rather than being miserable and doing nothing. And, above all, do not mask the pain or deny it by engaging in destructive behaviors—drugs, alcohol, overeating, promiscuous sex, life-threatening risks. Masked pain, or pain that is not dealt with, does not leave. It hangs around until you are willing to face it. Deal with your pain and it will leave. Hide from it and you will only produce more. Remember that you functioned before you fell in love and that you will function again after you fall out of love.

It may help to reverse the falling in love process. Conceptualize falling in love with the person as walking up a set of stairs. When we fall in love, we tend to overlook or disregard the things we do not like about the other. It is as if each time we walk up a stair, we throw something we do not like over the railing so that when we reach the top (being in love) we have thrown off all the negative traits and behaviors of the other. Falling out of love means walking down the same set of stairs and retrieving each of the things we threw over the railing. This time we focus on each thing that we did not like or that bothered us. Nothing is too small for our attention. When we get to the bottom of the stairs, we will be dealing with a flawed human being and this is someone that is easier to fall out of love with.

Try to avoid the romantic places and music that you have shared with the other. This is not the time for a trip down memory lane. Why bring on more pain than you already have? Put yourself in new environments or situations without painful memories. One day you will be able to hear "your songs" and be in "your places" and it will be bittersweet and you will more easily deal with it. But not now. Now it will only hurt like hell. Take good care of yourself.

Remember that when you are hurting and in pain, you need to be even kinder and more loving than usual to yourself. Avoid recriminations and self-blame and do not obsess over your past mistakes. You are human—imperfect—and you are allowed to make mistakes. You cannot maintain a relationship with the illusion of infallibility. When someone stops loving you, this has more to do with where they are than with what you have done. When you love others, your love is a gift to them. When you are loved, you are receiving a gift from someone else. You do not have any control over when and how others choose to give you their gifts. You cannot demand or expect these gifts because then they are no longer gifts. You can only expect the gift of being loved from yourself. When someone stops loving you, love yourself more. When you stop loving someone else, also love yourself more. This will help to reduce the neediness within yourself to be loved and will prevent symbiotic relationships with others.

What is good communication?

We have all heard that good communication is an important factor in relationships. We know that communication is comprised of talking but it is much more than just talking. There are too many couples who spend a large part of their lives together and talk a lot but do not feel that they are really communicating. Then there are the opposite couples who seem to talk very little but feel very close and connected. Communication is a means of obtaining intimacy with others. It is a way to share and to feel belongingness. Good communication allows others to really know us and to provide feedback and support when we need them. Good communication is one of the great joys of life. Practicing Social Interest involves learning good communication skills.

A key word in understanding good communication is the word *skills*. There are some lucky souls who naturally know how to communicate well with others but most of us have to learn these skills. Fortunately, they can be learned. A great paradox is that good communicators are always good listeners; they do not have to be good verbalizers. We have been taught to talk but we are generally never taught to listen. Effective listening is not always easy because it requires interest in the other and a great deal of concentration and patience. It is usually more fun to talk than it is to listen. The problem here is that most people want to have fun so there are not enough good listeners around. If we practice listening, really listening, to what others are saying, we may discover how unfamiliar this may feel. It takes skill to wait until they are totally finished with what they are saying and to concentrate on what they are saying rather than on what we want to say. We can learn to repeat back to them what we heard them say rather than assume that what we heard is what they said. It is difficult to stop our thinking and concentrate on listening. We may be amazed at how different this listening process feels.

Good communication also involves having a repertoire of both problem-solving and supportive skills. These are two different skills to be used at different times. You know problem-solving skills—these are what most of your communications are about. Someone talks about something and you give them your feedback —what you think and what you would do in their situation. For example: your partner says, "I'm so angry. I don't know what to do." You say, "I was also really angry today and so I decided to yell about it. Why don't you try yelling?" This is a problem-solving communication because you have told the other person what to do. Another example: your spouse says, "I'm late because I ran out of gas on the freeway." You say, "That was dumb. You should have filled up the tank before you left." Problem solving is a great form of communication when and only when someone asks you for your advice. The problems with problem-solving skills are that they are too easy and you probably overuse them. You may tend to rush in with advice long before you are asked for it. You most likely generalize this skill to almost all your communications and then may be surprised when people sometimes react negatively to you.

Supportive skills are more rare and tend to be much more difficult to learn. Supportive communication is the opposite of problem solving. You do not say what you think and you do not give advice unless you are specifically asked to do so. Even then, you find out what the other person is thinking about doing before you rush in with your ideas. Supportive communication means allowing the other person to feel good about solving the problem. If you think about most of our communications, you will discover that they are involved with demonstrating our own intelligence or abilities. Supportive communication shifts the onus of the conversation onto the other almost completely. It means allowing the other to say everything they want to say without interruptions or arguments. Supportive conversation first involves effective listening. It can also mean reflecting and repeating what the other has said. It also means objective listening and delaying your own needs in order to allow the other to express themselves. It means suspending judgment, presuppositions, and assumptions. No wonder it is so difficult. An example: your partner says, "I am so angry. I don't know what to do." As a supportive communicator, you may reply, "I hear you—you are angry" or you might say "What do you want to do?" or "Why are you angry?" or you might not say anything at all but express your interest nonverbally by stopping what you are doing and making direct eye contact and looking interested and objective. Support means that the other knows you are there with them and that you will listen and not attack them. Supportive communication is very powerful and requires Self-Esteem in order to do it well. You cannot be needy and also be supportive for very long. Sooner rather than later, your own needs will take over and you will want the focus of the communication to be on you. Supportive communications keep the focus of the conversation on the other person as long as they need it.

Therapists, consultants, nurses, and others involved in counseling and professionally helping people are lucky in that they learn supportive communication skills as part of their jobs. It is amazing how little we transfer this professional skill into our personal lives.

There is no more important place to practice being supportive than in the home environment. Here live the people that we love and that love us. And yet the home is without a doubt the most difficult place to practice being supportive.

Good communication would occur more often by changing the ratio of problem-solving and supportive communications. We probably use problem-solving skills about 90 percent of the time and supportive skills about 10 percent or less. If we could just flip this around to 90 percent supportive and less than 10 percent problem solving, we would have a great deal more Social Interest being demonstrated in the world. And we would all feel that we are being heard, that we share with others who care and that we belong.

V. The End

What is a "Natural High"?

As mentioned in the very beginning of this book, a *Natural High* is the end product from having Self-Esteem and Social Interest. Natural Highs are pure unadulterated joy at being alive. They reflect the love you have for yourself and the love you feel toward others. There is no other high in the world better than the Natural High. This is what you are experiencing when you feel united to everything and everyone. Some people describe Natural Highs as "feeling God" and others describe them as states of bliss. Natural Highs occur when you feel connected with the universe and when you feel that you are part of the whole. They occur when you recognize your own goodness (God within) and the goodness of others and the beauty that exists in the world (God outside). They occur spontaneously and sometimes in the strangest places at the oddest hours. They occur when you are open to the miracles around you and when you let go of your Weak Ego. Most children have Natural Highs because they are more easily in a state of grace.

Natural Highs never occur when you are focused on the past or the future. They require your presence in the moment. They do not occur because you want them to and they do not happen when you are working toward them. They are not a goal but a gift from God.

The very best way to experience Natural Highs is to practice Self-Esteem and Social Interest all of the time. That is an excellent way to be ready for them and open to the experience when it happens.

And it will happen to you if you let go and let it come. However, Natural Highs cannot occur when you are under the influence of an artificial high. When you are artificially high, you are trying to control feeling good and you are dependent on something outside of yourself to make you feel good. Natural Highs are about feeling good from being and are not in your control.

By accepting what you are, your humanness, by letting go of your needs and craziness, by experiencing the wonder of yourself and of others and by living in the moment without judgment or criticism, you leave yourself open to the Natural High. You are what you are. So be it. You are also more. So be it. Let go with love. You will experience your Natural High. You will be one with the Universe. You will belong. You will know your goodness and your Godliness.

Suggested Readings

PHILOSOPHICAL:

Campbell, Joseph. *The Power of Myth*. New York: Doubleday, 1988.

Castaneda, Carlos. *The Teachings of Don Juan: A Yaqui Way of Knowledge*. New York: Pocket Books, 1968. (All of the Don Juan series)

Golding, William. *Lord of the Flies*. New York: Coward-McCann, Inc., 1962.

Peck, M. Scott. *People of the Lie*. New York: Simon & Schuster, Inc., 1985.

Smith, Cyprian. *The Way of Paradox*. New York: Paulist Press, 1985.

Wilber, Ken. *No Boundary*. Boulder & London: Shambala, 1981.

SELF-ESTEEM:

Bradshaw, John. *Homecoming*. New York: Bantam Books, 1990.

O'Connell, Walter. *Super Natural Highs*. Chicago: North American Graphics, 1979.

Peck, M. Scott. *The Road Less Traveled.* New York: Simon & Schuster, Inc., 1978.

Yalom, Irvin D. *Love's Executioner and Other Tales of Psychotherapy.* New York: Basic Books, Inc., 1989.

SOCIAL INTEREST:

Beattie, Melody. *Beyond Codependency.* New York: Harper/Hazelden Books, 1989.

Greeley, Andrew M. *Sexual Intimacy: Love and Play.* New York: Warner Books, 1988.

Lazarus, Arnold A. *Marital Myths.* San Luis Obispo: Impact Publishers, 1988.

Biographical Sketch

Susanna McMahon

Educated at the University of Houston, Dr. Susanna McMahon has worked for the government in Texas and in Germany. She was director of the Community Mental Health Program in Madrid, Spain. She currently resides in Houston with her husband, J. Timothy McMahon, a management professor and consultant, and she writes, conducts workshops, and has a limited private practice. Her life is enriched by three adult daughters and three Spanish cats.